DEVOPS – A BUSINESS PERSPECTIVE

Other publications by Van Haren Publishing

Van Haren Publishing (VHP) specializes in titles on Best Practices, methods and standards within four domains:
- IT and IT Management
- Architecture (Enterprise and IT)
- Business Management and
- Project Management

Van Haren Publishing is also publishing on behalf of leading organizations and companies: ASLBiSL Foundation, BRMI, CA, Centre Henri Tudor, Gaming Works, IACCM, IAOP, IFDC, Innovation Value Institute, IPMA-NL, ITSqc, NAF, KNVI, PMI-NL, PON, The Open Group, The SOX Institute.

Topics are (per domain):

IT and IT Management	Enterprise Architecture	Project Management
ABC of ICT	ArchiMate®	A4-Projectmanagement
ASL®	GEA®	DSDM/Atern
CATS CM®	Novius Architectuur Methode	ICB / NCB
CMMI®		ISO 21500
COBIT®	TOGAF®	MINCE®
e-CF		M_o_R®
ISO/IEC 20000	**Business Management**	MSP®
ISO/IEC 27001/27002	BABOK® Guide	P3O®
ISPL	BiSL® and BiSL® Next	PMBOK® Guide
IT4IT®	BRMBOK™	Praxis®
IT-CMF™	BTF	PRINCE2®
IT Service CMM	EFQM	
ITIL®	eSCM	
MOF	IACCM	
MSF	ISA-95	
SABSA	ISO 9000/9001	
SAF	OPBOK	
SIAM™	SixSigma	
TRIM	SOX	
VeriSM™	SqEME®	

For the latest information on VHP publications, visit our website: www.vanharen.net.

DevOps

A Business Perspective

Oleg Skrynnik

Colophon

Title:	DevOps – A Business Perspective
Author:	Oleg Skrynnik
Text editor:	Roman Jouravlev
English translation:	Oleksandra Spiegler
Illustrations:	Oleg Skrynnik
Publisher:	Van Haren Publishing, 's-Hertogenbosch, www.vanharen.net
ISBN Hard copy:	978 94 018 0372 4
ISBN eBook:	978 94 018 0373 1
ISBN ePub:	978 94 018 0374 8
Edition:	First edition, first impression, December 2018
Lay-out and DTP:	Coco Bookmedia, Amersfoort – NL
Copyright:	© Van Haren Publishing

This book is a translation from original Russian version: DevOps для ИТ-менеджеров: Концентрированное структурированное изложение передовых идей, ISBN 978 5 00006 016 2

Trademarks:
COBIT© is a registered trademark of ISACA
ITIL© is a registered trademark of AXELOS Limited
SAFe© is a registered trademark of Scaled Agile, Inc.

All rights reserved. No part of this publication may be reproduced in any form by print, photo print, microfilm or any other means without written permission by the publisher.

Although this publication has been composed with much care, neither author, nor editor, nor publisher can accept any liability for damage caused by possible errors and/or incompleteness in this publication.

Despite the fact that the content of the book has been thoroughly prepared, the author and publisher do not bear any responsibility for possible damage suffered by someone due to errors or inaccuracies in the book.

Foreword

This book is written by an IT manager for IT specialists, IT managers and IT executives. It does not show DevOps as a phenomenon associated with new automation tools, programming techniques or technologies; it explains the management aspects of DevOps for those who are professionally engaged in information and technology *management*.

It differs from other books by the structural nature of the narrative (perhaps, excessively structured) and by the attempt to cover fully a phenomenon of DevOps at a basic, fundamental level. This does not mean that the narrative is superficial, sufficient just for creating awareness of the new subject area. 'Fundamental level' means building the foundation, the basics: I'm talking about the origins of DevOps; the inevitability of its emergence; the key prerequisites and their reflection in practices; about the practices themselves and the principles they are based upon.

Despite the abundance of literature on this subject, this is the very book I really missed when I myself studied DevOps. I aim to provide a clear, structured and concise review of this complex yet very interesting subject. I dare to hope that there are no superfluous words in this book, and on the contrary, all the necessary words are here.

I have to express my sincere thanks to my family and friends. I cannot say they helped me to write this book: fortunately, they have very little to do with such matters as DevOps. However, they definitely suffered from it: quite often, from July until December 2017, I went incommunicado and failed to react to their signals; sometimes I even demanded silence in evenings.

I also have to thank my colleagues at Cleverics. We established this business together with the brightest people I ever met, and it happened to be one of the most important decisions of my life. Common goals and principles; freedom in decision making; responsibility for the outcomes; and partners ready to support me when it is needed — without this I would not find time to structure my thinking on DevOps and to transform it into this book.

Finally, I thank our clients: they keep offering us new and exciting problems to solve; new challenges. They keep demanding new training, workshops and simulations; they want more and better… They literally do not allow us to stand still and constantly make us moving forward.

The author, Moscow, Autumn 2018

About this book

This book is the core literature of the EXIN DevOps Foundation certification. This exam tests the understanding of basic DevOps concepts and how they relate to each other, as well as the value of DevOps for the business. EXIN DevOps Foundation is the first level of the EXIN DevOps certification program. The EXIN DevOps Professional certification tests the knowledge of DevOps practices and how to integrate teams. The EXIN DevOps Master certification is about promoting organizational change and leading the way towards continuous delivery and improvement.

Acknowledgements

"I thought I knew a bit about DevOps these days, but I learned a lot from this book. It's in a narrative style, which I like. It comes from the perspective of legacy enterprise 'horses' moving to new ways of working, rather than a development technical focus. It hits all the points I would hit if I had ever gotten around to write such a book. I won't now, as Oleg has made such a good job of it. Well done!"

Rob England

"DevOps - A Business Perspective" is a well-written and carefully-curated summary of the key DevOps topics that IT managers should be aware of. It combines impartiality with astute and useful personal observations – the author clearly knows his stuff. I expect to be consulting it from time to time and I have no hesitation in recommending it."

Mark Smalley

"An easy to read and well thought out and constructed overview of the history of Devops in terms of practices and the accompanying technology. It offers some great summaries, poses dilemmas that organizations will face and gives some good examples on making choices for moving forward, at the same time signaling potential barriers and pitfalls to avoid. If you want a DevOps 101 this is it."

Paul Wilkinson

Contents

Acknowledgements — VII

1 What is DevOps? — 1
- 1.1 Origins — 3
  - 1.1.1 Agile methods for software development — 3
  - 1.1.2 Managing infrastructure as code — 7
  - 1.1.3 It was inevitable — 10
- 1.2 The definition — 10
- 1.3 Why DevOps? — 13
  - 1.3.1 Decrease time to market — 13
  - 1.3.2 Reduce technical debt — 17
  - 1.3.3 Eliminate fragility — 18
- 1.4 The history of origination — 20
- 1.5 Frequently expressed misconceptions — 22
  - 1.5.1 DevOps is a part of Agile — 22
  - 1.5.2 DevOps is all about tools and automation — 25
  - 1.5.3 DevOps is a new profession — 26
- 1.6 Summary — 27

2 The Foundation — 29
- 2.1 Lean production — 29
  - 2.1.1 Key facts — 29
  - 2.1.2 Challenges — 31
- 2.2 Agile — 33
  - 2.2.1 Key facts — 33
  - 2.2.2 Challenges — 34

3 The Principles — 37
- 3.1 Value stream — 37
- 3.2 Deployment pipeline — 40
- 3.3 Everything should be stored in a version control system — 44
- 3.4 Automated configuration management — 45
- 3.5 The Definition of Done — 46
- 3.6 Summary — 47

4 Key Practices 49

4.1 Key differences from traditional practices 49
4.1.1 Release is a routine 49
4.1.2 Release is a business decision 50
4.1.3 Everything is automated 52
4.1.4 Incidents are solved immediately 52
4.1.5 Defects are fixed immediately 53
4.1.6 Processes are improved continuously 54
4.1.7 Act as a startup 55
4.2 Unusual teams 56
4.3 Work visualization 59
4.4 Limit the WIP 62
4.5 Reduce batch size 66
4.6 Mind the operational requirements 67
4.7 Early detection and correction of defects 70
4.8 Controlled improvements and innovations 71
4.9 Funding that enables innovations 73
4.10 Task prioritization 76
4.11 Continual identification, exploitation and elevation of constraints 78
4.12 Summary 79

5 Practical Application 81

5.1 DevOps applicability and limitations 81
5.2 COTS 87
5.3 Evolving architecture 89
5.4 DevOps and ITSM 93
5.5 Cargo culting 96
5.6 Start where you are, progress iteratively 98
5.7 Value stream as the core 100
5.8 Summary 101

6 Conclusion 103

Appendices 105

Appendix 1 Test: Are you doing DevOps? 105
Appendix 2 Recommended reading 109

About the author 110

Index 111

1 What is DevOps?

Methods of IT management do not stand still. Approaches to the development and operation of information systems nowadays are different from those several decades ago. Moreover, tomorrow will be the time of the next generation of refined methods and techniques, which will be based on new knowledge, experience and technology. Most of the time, management methods evolve gradually, by means of systematizing and honing of the models created earlier, based on certain basic principles and postulates. However, from time to time, discontinuities occur, allowing individual leader organizations to make a significant step forward with regards to effective and efficient use of information technology.

A good example is the transition of IT management from focus on IT systems to managing IT services. Having started around the year 2000, this change in the view of management enabled pioneers to gain significant competitive advantages. Successfully adopted by the leaders, emerging management practices became so-called best practices; and some of the best practices evolved further to generally accepted good practices, and even contributed to industry standards. Of course, some organizations did not use the best practices or standards in their work: not all spheres of economy were significantly IT-dependent in those days.

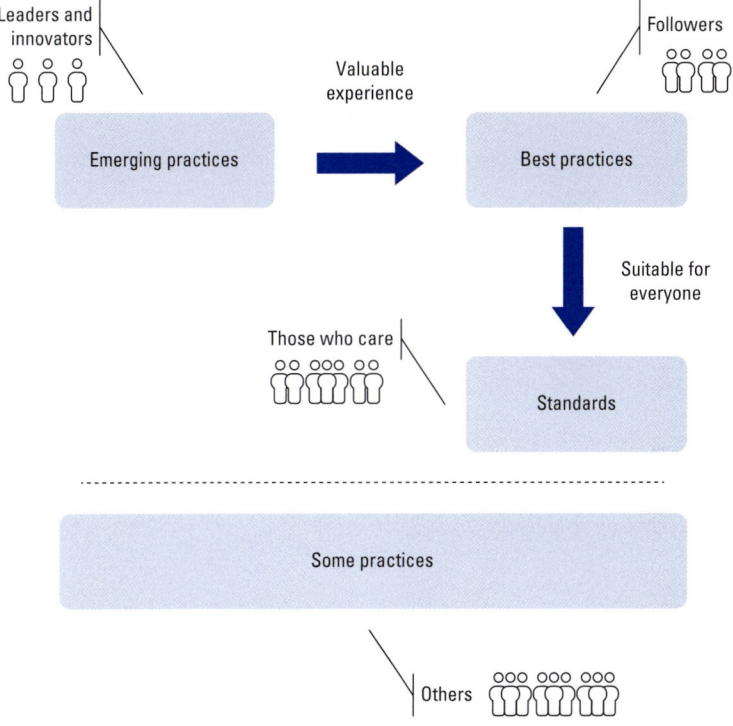

Fig. 1.1   Emergence and use of new practices

Let us look at IT service management, for example. In the 1980s, the idea to provide value from information technology in the form of services and to organize IT activities in the form of processes arose. Certain European companies became pioneers, developing new practices in organizing work and approaches to solving management problems. Some of the practices, such as introduction of a Service Desk; distinction between incidents and problems; managed and controlled processing of IT infrastructure changes, etc., were formulated in 2000-2001 in key publications such as ITIL® (it used to stand for *IT Infrastructure library* in those days)[1]. This allowed them to move into the category of best practices, and not only leading organizations, but also the 'followers' started using them. Eventually, in the year 2002 BS 15000-1:2002, the first standard for IT service management was published, which established a certain norm to be followed by those who seek to build a coherent IT service management system. That said, practices, publications and standards do not stop developing:

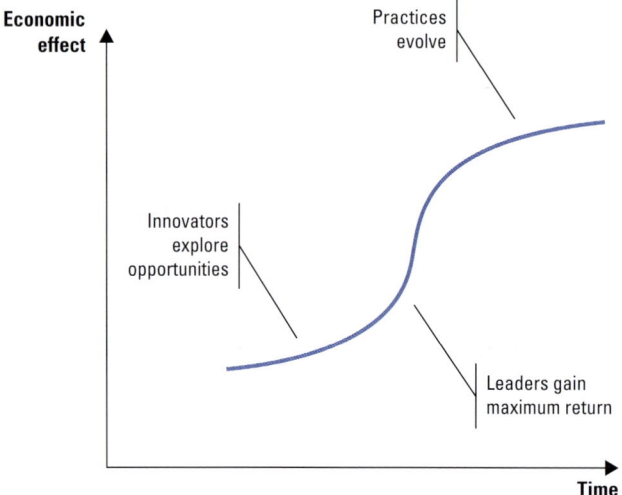

Fig. 1.2   Development of practices

Similar dynamics can be observed now in Agile software development. However, the revolution that is brewing here affects a larger area than software development alone and the scale of the consequences may be on the same level as that of ITSM.

New, emerging practices have been labelled 'DevOps' (Development + Operations), which is as far from the intended meaning as ITIL® is far from the concept of 'library', and today's COBIT from control objectives.

---

1   https://www.axelos.com/best-practice-solutions/itil

> While publishing COBIT 5 in 2012, the copyright holder pointed out that, even though originally COBIT was an abbreviation of 'Control Objectives for Information and Related Technology', now it is a just proper name[2].
>
> ITIL® custodian since 2013, AXELOS Limited has made similar comments about ITIL®.
>
> DevOps experts, who were the originators of this movement, acknowledge the limited nature of the name, calling to use more accurate in their opinion 'BizDevOps', 'DevSecOps' and the like. However, the probability of changing the name is now insignificant.

So, the DevOps phenomenon is worth studying. To understand fully the essence of DevOps, it is necessary to consider the background of both the idea and the movement associated with it.

1.1 Origins

One could argue that DevOps appeared due to two factors: wide adoption of agile software development methods and of management of IT infrastructure as a program code. Let's look at each of them.

1.1.1 Agile methods for software development

At the end of the 20th century, the dominant methodology of software development was the so-called 'waterfall model': sequential execution of predetermined stages, each of which takes significant time and ends with the achievement of previously agreed results; transition to the next stage in many cases occurs only after the previous stage is fully and formally completed. An additional distinguishing feature of this model is the functional specialization of the people involved at each stage: analysts, architects, developers, testers, and so on.

When developing large information systems of pre-defined functionality and with no or limited requirements for fast delivery of the product, this model enables creation of high-quality products, combined with effective and detailed cost control.

However, at the end of the 1990s, with the rapid growth of Internet technologies and web programming, downsides of the waterfall model started to affect interaction and understanding between information systems customers (internal or external business) and providers (internal or external software developers). Indeed, emerging market opportunities available for business customers required rapid launches (within a few months) of new products to the market. However, a typical development cycle from the

---

[2] http://www.isaca.org/COBIT/Pages/FAQs.aspx

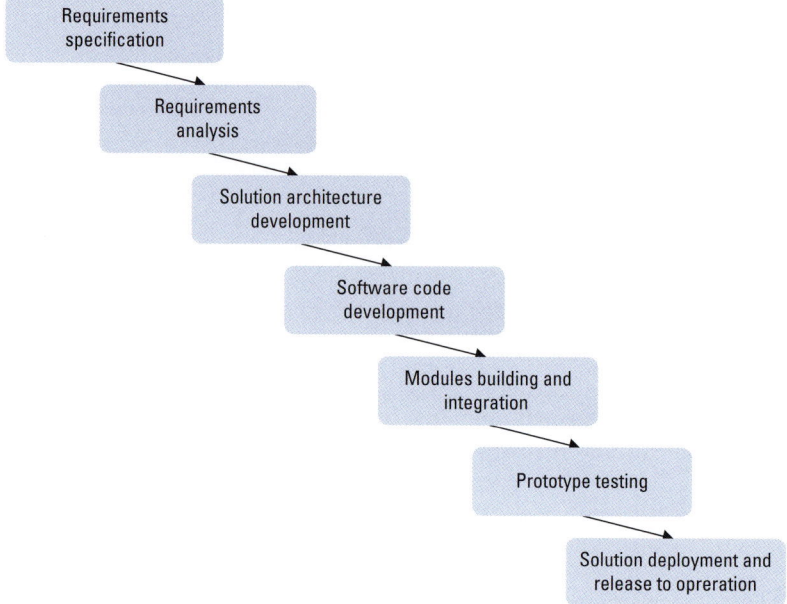

Fig. 1.3   An example of a waterfall software development model

beginning of the project to the first working prototype could take from six to 18 months; up to 2-3 years in larger enterprises. In addition, with the emergence of previously unknown but potentially promising market opportunities, customer requirements could change in the course of the development, which was extremely difficult to take into account without extending the deadlines, or reducing the quality of the product.

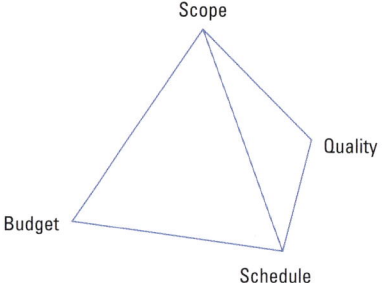

Fig. 1.4   Classical pyramid of the project management constraints

Thus, tension was building up between customers and providers; between the core business and software developers. Innovative approaches to programming were the answer to this challenge. Ken Schwaber published several books about Scrum[3]. Kent Beck published a book on extreme programming, or XP[4]. However, the effect of the application

---

3   For example: Schwaber, K., *Agile Software Development with Scrum*, 2001, ISBN: 978-0130676344
4   Beck, K., *Extreme Programming Explained: Embrace Change*, 1999, ISBN 978-0201616415; 2nd edition, 2004, 978-0134052021

of these new ideas was moderate, mainly because it was focused on just one of the stages of the software development cycle — the actual programming, while the problem was wider. The end-to-end software development cycle needed to be simplified and speeded up.

In 2001, Schwaber and Beck, along with fifteen other experts, met up to discuss the existing problems and to work out a solution. The outcome of the meeting was the so-called Agile Manifesto. It was designed to bridge the gap between business and software developers. One of the manifesto's authors, Robert C. Martin, explains[5]:

'Trust between developers and business can emerge and develop when the right disciplines and the right minimum process are used. Business will start to trust the developers, instead of thinking that they are lazy, corrupt, nasty creatures, and the developers will start to pay attention to business and realize that they are reasonable and rational beings, rather than someone from another planet.'

The subsequent developing and adoption of agile methods by the community of programmers and project managers greatly accelerated and restructured software development.

Agile Manifesto[6]

We are uncovering better ways of developing software by doing it and helping others do it. Through this work, we have come to value:

Individuals and interactions	over	processes and tools
Working software	over	comprehensive documentation
Customer collaboration	over	contract negotiation
Responding to change	over	following a plan

That is, while there is value in the items on the right side, we value the items on the left more.

We follow these principles:
1. Our highest priority is to satisfy the customer through early and continuous delivery of valuable software.
2. Welcome changing requirements, even late in development. Agile processes harness change for the customer's competitive advantage.
3. Deliver working software frequently, from a couple of weeks to a couple of months, with a preference to the shorter timescale.

---

5 https://www.youtube.com/watch?v=hG4LH6P8Syk, also https://www.aaron-gray.com/a-criticism-of-scrum/
6 http://agilemanifesto.org/iso/en/manifesto.html

4. Business people and developers must work together daily throughout the project.
5. Build projects around motivated individuals. Give them the environment and support they need, and trust them to get the job done.
6. The most efficient and effective method of conveying information to and within a development team is face-to-face conversation.
7. Working software is the primary measure of progress.
8. The sponsors, developers, and users should be able to maintain a constant pace indefinitely. Agile processes promote sustainable development.
9. Continuous attention to technical excellence and good design enhances agility.
10. Simplicity — the art of maximizing the amount of work not done — is essential.
11. The best architectures, requirements, and designs emerge from self-organizing teams.
12. At regular intervals, the team reflects on how to become more effective, then tunes and adjusts its behavior accordingly.

The key elements of agile development are: closer interaction between the customer and the developer, reduction of the batch size, products delivered at short intervals (cycles) and limited size of the teams.

Using an agile approach, the software development team releases a new viable product every two to four weeks. End users are closely involved in the development, thus ensuring fast feedback, which, in turn, inspires faster changes.

However, in many companies, abandoning the waterfall model in favour of agile development, effect was smaller than expected. Failure to benefit from agile observed in many companies, often has little to do with advantages of the waterfall model or the disadvantages of agile. The problem roots in the fact that development of the code is only one of the links in a long value chain.

Indeed, prior to the development there is still a significant group of steps aimed at identifying business needs, their elaboration, analysis, prioritization, and so on.

Furthermore, after development, applications need to be quickly deployed in the production environment, so that the customers received all the benefits they had been promised, and could provide feedback to the developers. However, IT infrastructure of almost every organization established before 2010 is based on rigid, expensive hardware procured a long time ago; budgets for it were obtained with great difficulty and the budgeting process for new procurement is lengthy.

Moreover, this infrastructure is in a rather fragile state in a large number of organizations. One of the factors contributing to such fragility is that the IT solutions used are extremely complex. There are many thousands of interconnected items in the infrastructure. Another contributor is the lack of IT systems documentation, as well as the rapid obsolescence of the documentation. The latter is continually enhanced by the loss of knowledge due to the staff turnover.

In many organizations it is unsafe to touch IT infrastructure. Change is the biggest evil for IT operations department, and a constant large flow of changes may lead to truly catastrophic consequences.

Thus, advanced methods of software development are held up by obstacles on the IT operations side, which decreases the possible positive effect of applying agile approaches.

> To deal with IT infrastructure fragility, some organizations use formalized and automated change management process designed to structure the flow of changes and minimize the risks associated with their implementation,

1.1.2 Managing infrastructure as code

The emergence of management of IT infrastructure as code was preceded by development of two technologies: virtualization and cloud computing.

The history of virtualization of software and hardware environments began quite a long time ago, in 1964, with the beginning of the development of the IBM CP-40 operating system[7]. During the years of consistent development of this area, considerable progress has been made. First commercially available systems for mainframes appeared in the 1970s, and those for subsequently more common machines based on the Intel x86 architecture appeared in the 1980s[8]. The chart below shows the number of key events related to virtualization between 1964 and 2008 (the graph does not stop at this year by accident, as you will see further):

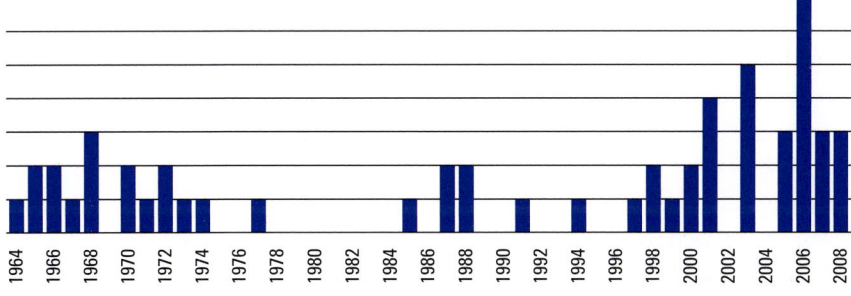

Fig. 1.5 Key virtualization events distributed in time

---

7   https://en.wikipedia.org/wiki/IBM_CP-40
8   It is interesting to note that, according to Jez Humble, in those years during a certain period of time IBM avoided recommending virtualization products to its customers, as this affected the sales of the hardware.

Virtualization made it possible not only to use expensive and powerful hardware more efficiently, but also to introduce an additional level of abstraction between the executable code that provides something useful to the customer and the underlying system software. A significant step was taken in the direction of separating the competences and responsibilities of, so to speak, 'application engineers' and 'system engineers', in the broad sense of these concepts.

Cloud computing technology developed even faster. Until the middle of the 1990s, telecommunication companies offered their customers the Wide Area Network (WAN) service by connecting the relevant endpoints, for each customer with direct cabling. However, with the emergence of private virtual network technology (VPN, Virtual Private Network), it became possible to send data packets of different clients via the same data transmission channels, providing the necessary level of security, privacy and quality of service. At that time providers started to use the cloud symbol to show the border between the client's private network and the shared network, and the respective separation of responsibility.

With the new capability of transferring data over long distances, customers started using these technologies not only for the information exchange between their remote systems, but also for distributing the computational load between different nodes of their networks. The emergence of a technology to simplify and cheapen this interaction was prompted. Small providers took the first steps, but truly significant changes happened in 2006, when Amazon presented ECC (Elastic Compute Cloud). Soon, in 2008, Microsoft launched its service, Azure, and Google introduced the Google App Engine, subsequently evolved into the Google Cloud Platform. Of course, these are not the only examples of renting out the computing capacity, but they are the largest ones.

Virtualization and cloud technologies have significantly changed the computing landscape. Resources offered by commercial providers have become affordable and reliable; they also assured the necessary level of security. The customers' attitude to the clouds and their use has changed from *"someone else is controlling my hardware somewhere"* to *"I have an infrastructure that I manage remotely"*.

> The US National Institute of Standards and Technology identified five essential characteristics of cloud computing[9]:
> 1. On-demand self-service. A consumer can unilaterally provision computing capabilities, such as server time and network storage, as needed automatically without requiring human interaction with each service provider.

---

9   http://nvlpubs.nist.gov/nistpubs/Legacy/SP/nistspecialpublication800-145.pdf

2. Broad network access. Capabilities are available over the network and accessed through standard mechanisms that promote use by heterogeneous thin or thick client platforms.
3. Resource pooling. The provider's computing resources are pooled to serve multiple consumers using a multi-tenant model, with different physical and virtual resources dynamically assigned and reassigned according to consumer demand.
4. Rapid elasticity. Capabilities can be elastically provisioned and released, in some cases automatically, to scale rapidly outward and inward commensurate with demand. To the consumer, the capabilities available for provisioning often appear to be unlimited and can be appropriated in any quantity at any time.
5. Measured service. Cloud systems automatically control and optimize resource use by leveraging a metering capability at some level of abstraction appropriate to the type of service.

What does managing the infrastructure remotely mean? Let's recall one of the key paradigms of UNIX-systems: all the necessary actions with the system should be accessible from the command line (hence, using a script). Graphical user interfaces are a beautiful, but optional.

Now, let us combine the virtual cloud technologies and the command line interface for all tasks. As a result, IT professionals could create the parts of the IT infrastructure they needed, including servers, storage systems, and network components, and all interfaces between them, all settings and configurations by means of the of text commands... The degree of automation has increased significantly, and so has the speed of the change implementation. Previously, to deploy an IT infrastructure based on in-house hardware, it was required:
- to justify and agree a budget (weeks and months);
- to wait for the next purchase cycle (months);
- to order equipment from the supplier and pay for it (days);
- to wait for delivery (weeks and months);
- to receive, install, configure, prepare for use (days and weeks).

Today it is possible to create a similar IT infrastructure by:
- running a script, waiting for completion of its execution (minutes, rarely hours);
- clearing the invoice from the cloud provider at the end of the month.

That is, the required infrastructure is created using the program code. It not only is created, but also can be managed as a program code: with version control, change tracking, debugging, reusing previous versions and so on. These aspects will be discussed in more detail Chapter 3 *The Principles*.

To conclude the picture, I also want to acknowledge the second life, which some relatively old technologies have obtained. For example, virtualization at the operating system level was available in many UNIX-systems in the 1980s. However, the serious commercial success of this technology, which is often called containerization, came only in the second half of the period 2000-2010, coinciding with the events described above. While the original *chroot* mechanism was rather limited in functionality and capabilities, now it is possible to isolate a file system for containers, allocate disk quotas, limit the RAM available, or processor time, I/O bandwidth and so on.

1.1.3 It was inevitable

> "Somebody is saying this is inevitable — and whenever you hear somebody saying that, it's very likely to be a set of businesses campaigning to make it true".
>
> Richard Stallman, founder of Free Software Foundation and creator of the GNU operating system, on cloud computing[10], 2008

Having reviewed the origins of DevOps, we can draw the following conclusions.

First, due to the emergence of new ways of interacting with the business customers, and to the adequate application of agile development techniques, *a need* for new ways of IT management has developed.

Second, with the emergence of new infrastructure management technologies, it became *possible* to organize the IT work differently.

Taking a realistic look at R. Stallman's words quoted above (it seems like he was mistaken about the cloud computing), one can assume that the emergence of something similar to DevOps was only a matter of time.

1.2 The definition

Only very self-confident or infinitely incompetent people, as well as generally recognized gurus, can seriously discuss a phenomenon without giving it a definition, or without relying on a generally accepted definition. Unfortunately, the situation is far from simple with DevOps.

Some experts try to make up something of their own, close to their understanding. Others argue that it is impossible to determine DevOps at the moment, since it is rather

---

10 https://www.theguardian.com/technology/2008/sep/29/cloud.computing.richard.stallman

a phenomenon, a movement, an idea, but not a discipline or a methodology. Still others say that everyone has their own DevOps, and offer a well-known metaphor of the blind men touching an elephant: one says that it is most likely a tree, another — that it feels like a rug, the third one says that it is snake-like, and so on.

Researching this topic, I managed to read a large number of books and online publications, to communicate with various people involved in the DevOps movement, both in Russia and in Europe, to attend specialized training courses and to pass several international exams. In my opinion, the impossibility of defining DevOps is somewhat exaggerated. Of course, so many men, so many opinions, and in case of consultants it gets more out of hand: two consultants means at least three opinions. However, having a systemic mindset, a degree in IT and consultancy experience in the field of IT management, I found it possible to approach the issue in a clear and structured manner. Without claiming it to be universal or the ultimate truth, I put together the following definition:

DevOps is an evolution of the ideas of agile software development and lean manufacturing, applied to the end-to-end value chain in IT, which allows businesses to achieve more with modern information technologies due to cultural, organizational and technical changes

There are four important points that need to be emphasized in this definition.

First, it seems important to point out that DevOps does not replace agile and lean practices, but kind of absorbs them. My communication with colleagues, clients, and training attendees shows that those who are not familiar with Agile development, discover a lot of new and interesting things in DevOps. Those who have relevant training and experience are surprised by the number of overlaps between DevOps and other practices, such as Lean, Scrum and Kanban. In my opinion, it is not entirely correct to call this phenomenon an 'overlap'. Rather, it is about borrowing and expanding the ideas of agile development and lean manufacturing. This matter will be discussed in more detail in Chapter 2 *The Foundation*.

Second, the very essence of DevOps lies in the fact that the IT department together with the business think not only about software development, but also about the whole value chain. This chain begins with the generation of new ideas together with business stakeholders, and proceeds through development, testing, deployment, down to operation. This approach promotes analysis, identifications and elimination of bottlenecks in the end-to-end value chain. It establishes feedback loops not only from the end of the chain to its beginning, but also between the steps, as well as within every step. DevOps pays maximum attention to these elements: system approach, work with constraints and feedback enablement. This will be described in detail below.

Third, it is important to emphasize the expected value from using DevOps, which lies in greater return on information technology. According to the classical view, information technologies allow organizations to get more benefits (by creating new opportunities or eliminating existing constraints), to reduce risks and to optimize resources. Properly used, DevOps addresses all three of these aspects. It would be incorrect to say that organizations cannot benefit from information technology in traditional ways, without DevOps. However, DevOps provides *greater* value, which can be expressed in accelerating the delivery of the new and modified products to the market; quicker response to customer needs; improved availability and sustainability of IT systems; more efficient use of limited resources. This topic will be presented in more details in Section 1.3 *Why DevOps?*.

Lastly, in the final part of the definition, there are explicit indications of the three essential elements: cultural, organizational and technical means. In fact, this is the old mantra of processes, people and technology. The experience of the DevOps pioneers, as well as their followers, shows that its importance is still high.

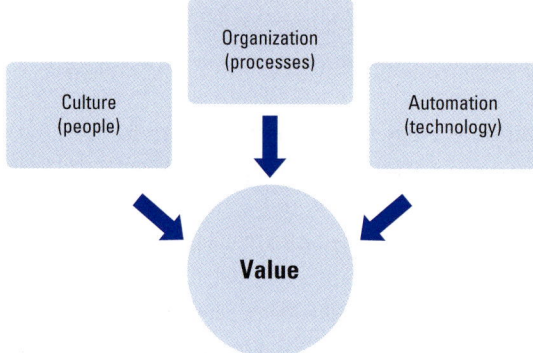

Fig. 1.6   Three essential elements

Here is the DevOps definition with a breakdown into the components, which allows emphasizing the key points:

DevOps is
a. an evolution of the ideas of agile software development and lean manufacturing,
b. applied to the end-to-end value chain in IT,
c. which allows businesses to achieve more with modern information technologies,
d. due to cultural, organizational and technical changes.

1.3 Why DevOps?

> "Listen, if stars are lit, it means there is someone who needs it."
>
> V. Mayakovsky[11], 1914

Some management frameworks emerge as a product of the author's (perhaps an expert's, or even a guru's) imagination: a kind of theoretical research. Their applicability, or inapplicability, is proven by adherents and followers trying to use new techniques in their work and in managing others.

Other approaches are born as a response to quite pressing needs. They are created not by the order of the British Crown and not by groups of specially recruited consultants. These approaches are developed by practitioners seeking ways to eliminate certain difficulties or constraints; or to make the use of available limited resources more efficient; or to create new businesses, new niches, and new tools to solve specific (and real) problems.

It seems that DevOps is closer to the second group, rather than to the first one. Details of its origination has been discussed in Section 1.4 *The history of origination*; for now, let's focus on the main problems that various organizations are trying to solve with the help of DevOps.

1.3.1 Decrease time to market

Companies using DevOps most often report the need to reduce significantly time to market. Different people mean different things by this term. A common understanding is the time from the inception of a business idea to the possibility for a customer to purchase a new product or to get a new service as a result of this business idea being realized. Thus, a calculation (or rather an assessment) of the time to market deals with a fairly large time frame. In case of IT department being involved, this time frame consists of the following steps:

- structuring and initial formal drafting of a business idea, or rather several business ideas, and their justification;
- evaluation and selection of a business idea for implementation;
- planning of the actions required for implementation; obtaining funds;
- staff and business processes preparation;
- at the same time: formalization of requirements, prototype development, initial testing, development of a fully-featured IT system, its thorough testing, release and deployment;

---

11 Vladimir Mayakovsky, *Listen! Early Poems*, translation by Maria Enzenberger, City Lights Books, 1991, ISBN 978-0872862555

- at the same time: marketing activities, preparation of the market, preparation of the sales channels and tools;
- a new product or service launch.

The described process introduces certain challenges. First, it can take years, while the business would like to reduce it to months. The business justification for urgency here is transparent: during the development of a new product, the market can change so much that the product itself will no longer be relevant, or competitors will release a similar product earlier, take the cream and become the leaders. Early entry into the market with an attractive competitive offer helps gaining a dominant position in new niches, which in turn gives the leader an opportunity to further change the market, adjusting it for themselves. This is an essential advantage that only few have, but everyone is aiming for. In addition, we should not forget about the ever-increasing rate of change. One of the best illustrations of this thesis is the Law of Accelerating Returns, formulated in 1999 by Ray Kurzweil [12]. According to it, the rate of change in a wide range of evolving systems, including, but not limited to new technologies, tends to grow exponentially. In practice, this means that breakthroughs in technology, including information, happen more often. Companies that *increase* the pace of change become leaders, and those who can only *keep* their fast pace, get a chance not to stay on the side-lines. What can be said about those who cannot change quickly…

> "It is hard to be a film script writer. One cannot keep up with the circumstances that change at lightning speed. … First you write the script, then it's rehearsed, then it's handed over to the distribution offices and only then it reaches the screen. At this point, something new and more relevant to the moment comes out…
>
> The authors … of different and topical plays are in exactly the same position. They will soon have to write while having their morning coffee, reading newspapers. So that by noon the play is ready for the dress rehearsal, and in the evening it is shown to the public. Only under this indispensable condition can they catch the moment."
>
> From: *The Theatre*, Moscow daily theatre newspaper[13],
> August 1917

The second difficulty of the process described above is the need for clear coordination and harmonization of interdependent steps, especially those that are carried out simultaneously. At this point, many companies fall into the classic trap: while there is no end product ready, there is nothing to advertise and sell, but when it emerges, marketing activities lead to sales (hence the financial returns) only with a delay. This trap further

---

12 http://www.kurzweilai.net/the-law-of-accelerating-returns
13 https://project1917.ru/groups/teatr

increases the actual time to market and requires everyone's work to be coordinated even more carefully.

Note that the role of the traditional IT department in increasing the time to market can hardly be overestimated. Indeed, in some organizations, from the total time to market duration of 1.5 to 2 years, IT accounts for more than 50% to 70%.

Another understanding of the term 'time to market' is less global, but not less significant. Dynamic companies that create digital products are used to acting quickly. They prefer safe-to-fail experiments to scrupulous and detailed planning, and the word *idea* is replaced by a *hypothesis*. In this case, the process looks like this:
- creation of a hypothesis, development of the validation methods;
- practical implementation of the hypothesis;
- result evaluation, A/B testing, comparison with targets;
- adjustment based on the analysis, return to the first or second step.

It is easy to see a cycle here; its expected duration is weeks. This fast pace is necessary because the very essence of this movement is in constant search. At the start, at the very beginning, the final state is completely unknown, and so is the road to it. Long-term planning does not make any sense, the company sees only the next, the proximate step; or, to be more precise, it tries to guess it. A well-known metaphor to illustrate this thesis compares the survival and development of a business with exploration of a money river. Having entered this river once, having found a new niche and new opportunities, the company will need to keep exploring the changing river bed. While traditional processes, regulations, and already existing products are likely to increase the inertia of the company, if left unattended, they will lead to the shore with no money on it.

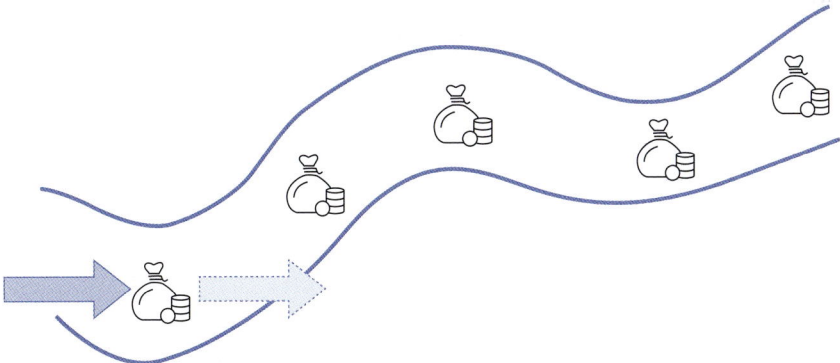

Fig. 1.7   The Money river

It is not hard to guess that the contribution of the IT department to the slowing down of the above cycle is high. Indeed, the role of IT is key in creation of digital products, so the delays in the implementation phase of the hypothesis are most likely due to the 'slow' IT department taking months instead of the expected weeks.

To reduce the time to market, DevOps offers a variety of techniques, for example: reducing the batch size, reducing the number of handoffs, continual identification and elimination of losses, and others. They will be looked into in more detail in Chapter 4 *Key Practices*. Now, it is important to note the following: it is naïve to hope that using DevOps techniques to accelerate the work of IT department will simultaneously lead to a reduction in IT costs. Rather, the cost of information technology will grow, primarily, due to the increase in the number of IT staff. Indeed, the traditional organization of the IT department assumes separate functional units, each of which deals with all tasks within its subject area (business analysis, development and testing, operation, support, and so on). At the same time, within each functional unit, the necessary interchangeability of specialists is ensured, and the significant number of specialists of the same qualifications and competences makes it possible to distribute the workload evenly.

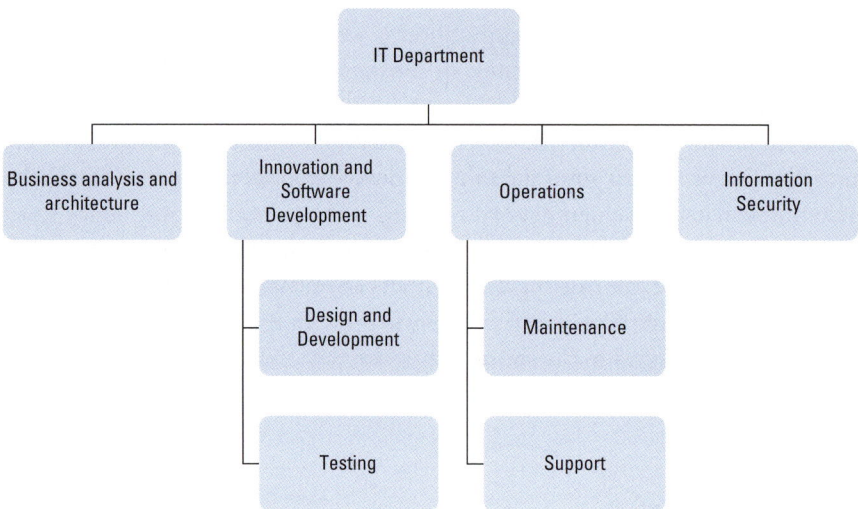

Fig. 1.8 Functional structure of a traditional IT unit

Unlike this scheme, DevOps groups specialists into dedicated product teams. Each self-sufficient team includes a product owner, architects, developers, testers, and specialists responsible for operation, and for information security. With a large number of teams, focused exclusively on their product, it is more difficult to assure that the workload is even; it can lead to underutilization, and hence to higher costs of the human resources (this topic will be continued in Section 4.2 *Unusual teams*).

Thus, it can be argued that the traditional IT unit follows 'Optimize for cost' model, while the DevOps organization is aimed at 'Optimize for speed' model and these goals are generally contradictory. Note also that DevOps offers tools and techniques to limit

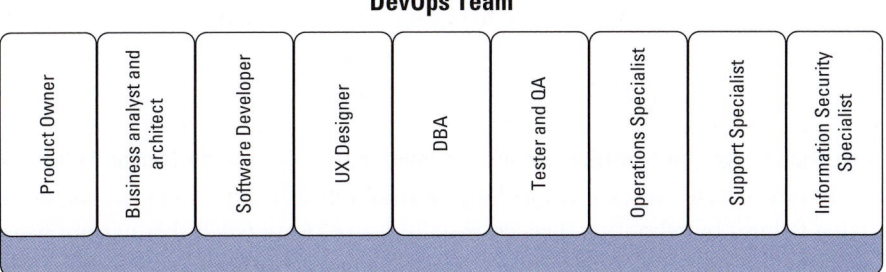

Fig. 1.9   Example of a DevOps team

the increase of costs, such as the automation of all routine operations, or specialists' interchangeability within the teams. In addition, DevOps adepts rightly point out that speed optimization in many cases is aimed at enabling the business to earn more, which compensates for the rising costs of IT. In this case, IT department is treated as a true business partner, not the cost centre.

1.3.2   Reduce technical debt

The concept of technical debt was proposed by Ward Cunningham in 1992[14]. The debt occurs when a programmer chooses a non-optimal way to solve a problem in order to shorten the development time. Cunningham noted that this is a natural process, and the problem is that accumulated non-optimal solutions lead to a gradual deterioration in the development outputs, and, as a consequence, to degrading product quality. Over time, development team will have to devote more resources to fix the consequences of earlier decisions, that is, refactoring the existing code, rather than developing new functionality. The analogy with the financial debt in this case is very clear: to speed up the output, the company can 'get into debts', but it should not allow the situation when all the revenue is spent on debt servicing.

Martin Fowler further developed the idea of technical debt by proposing a classification of the reasons for its occurrence[15]:

	Reckless	Prudent
Deliberate	"We don't have time for design"	"We must ship now and deal with consequences
Inadvertent	"What's layering?"	"Now we know how we should have done it"

Fig. 1.10   Technical debt quadrant by Martin Fowler

---

14 http://wiki.c2.com/?WardExplainsDebtMetaphor
15 https://martinfowler.com/bliki/TechnicalDebtQuadrant.html

His point of view generally reiterates the thought of Ward Cunningham: in a properly organized development team, increasing technical debt can be a conscious step to obtain short-term benefits; it is important to pay attention to paying the debt off.

At present, the concept of technical debt is usually applied in a wider sense. With the expansion to operational issues, a whole layer of traditional IT department problems is raised: fixing failures by rebooting devices; installing a software patch that has not been properly tested; IT infrastructure changes implementation without careful planning; manual patching or server configuration without documenting the changes — these are just some examples of accumulating technical debt, which nobody in a regular IT department will ever 'pay off'. Some IT organizations do not even plan for such works or projects, others entertain illusions of putting things in order, as soon as there is a spare minute for this. Of course, there is no spare minute in a modern IT department.

Moreover, it can be argued that some well-known practices offered by ITIL®, when applied inexpertly or in isolation, can also lead to growth of technical debt. For example, the incident management process according to ITIL® does not have the purpose of finding and eliminating the causes of failures. Its objective is to restore the IT system (or IT service, the difference is not material here) as soon as possible, often by using workarounds and temporary fixes. The use of such solutions nearly guarantees that failures will happen again; hence the new IT costs for their re-elimination. ITIL® authors assumed that problem management would work together with incident management process, aiming to identify and eliminate the root causes of incidents: in fact, to reduce technical debt in its broadest sense. However, we note that while in most modern IT departments there is at least some practice of incident management, it is extremely difficult to trace effective problem management process in the wild.

DevOps pays close attention to reducing technical debt, or rather managing it. Here are just two of the commonly used practices. First, constant refactoring of the program code allows to take into account the experience gained in the operation, and the work on eliminating previously created (consciously or accidentally) bottlenecks is planned on a par with the creation of new functionality. Second, DevOps strongly recommends using the practice of 'facing the issues as frequent as possible' in order to prevent 'stagnation' of problems that everyone knows about, but no one can get their hands on.

1.3.3 Eliminate fragility

As mentioned in *Agile methods for software development*, IT infrastructure of most organizations is in a very fragile state. This is due to many combined factors:
- technical solutions were created gradually, for years, from different components;
- large third-party systems are used, highly customized for the company's objectives;
- legacy systems of in-house development are used, while key programmers and teams may no longer work in the company;

- a large number of systems are integrated among themselves, as well as with external data sources and consumers, in a very complicated way;
- quality of the solutions is often suboptimal because of the need for faster implementation, as well as budget constraints;
- maintenance and support practices add temporary workarounds, 'crutches', just to keep the lights on;
- documentation of program code, architecture, infrastructure, technical solutions and even contractual obligations leaves much to be desired.

Gene Kim, Jez Humble, Patrick Debois and John Willis note[16] that ironically the most important and business beneficial systems in organizations are the most fragile ones. Reducing the fragility of these systems is extremely difficult because of the high risks of business disruption, zero tolerance to downtimes, and the constant flow of new changes and improvements related specifically to these systems.

However, to continue working with such an unstable infrastructure is dangerous for the IT managers' career. Besides, in addition to long-term impending troubles, there are operational difficulties. Making any changes is a risk, and therefore, appropriate tools to reduce it are needed: a long and thorough justification of every change, planning, negotiation and approval, development, testing and, finally, implementation. All this significantly slows down implementation of changes, and negatively affects the ability of IT organization to innovate.

DevOps offers to combat the fragility of IT systems in the most radical way: through its total elimination. In the traditional paradigm, the new code is inoperative until testing proves it is working. By contrast, in DevOps both the code and the system as a whole are fully functional at any one time, and if the next change disrupts their performance, it immediately rolls back and the system continues to work properly.

In his book *Antifragile: Things That Gain from Disorder*[17] Nassim Taleb discusses the characteristics of complex systems and introduces the following classification: fragile systems, resilient systems and antifragile systems. This classification helps to choose an approach to work: fragile systems first and foremost need stability, they need to be changed as little as possible, and changes should be carefully checked both before and after the intervention. Resilient systems are designed with regards to their inherent complexity and fragility; mechanisms for fault tolerance and survival are put in place and they allow to worry less about possible negative impact of failures. However, the so-called antifragile systems that evolve when affected by malfunctions and disorder are even closer to being perfect. And disorder is the everyday reality of corporate information technology.

---

16 Kim, G., J. Humble, P. Debois, J. Willis, *The Devops Handbook: How to Create Worldclass Agility Reliability and Security in Technology Organizations*, 2016, ISBN 978-1942788003
17 Taleb, N., *Antifragile: Things That Gain from Disorder*, 2012, ISBN 978-1400067824

One of the great practices of DevOps related to antifragility is the deliberate introduction of chaos and instability into production environment. This technique is known by various names: Game Day, Chaos Monkey, Simian Army, but the essence remains unchanged. Specially developed software disrupts operation of IT systems, servers, data transmission and storage systems, and so on, randomly at unknown times. Target IT systems must respond in an independent and prompt manner to detect a fault and restore their normal operation, ideally in such a way that the end users notice nothing, and the data, of course, are not lost. This technique can be tried in a traditional IT department, but in many companies it may lead to a complete business disruption.

So, we have examined three main tasks DevOps is expected to address: reducing time to market, reducing technical debt and eliminating fragility. Each of them, solved individually, can give significant advantages to modern business, but the three together represent a powerful driver for changes. Examination of each of the tasks ended with a brief description of the relevant DevOps practices. We should note now that the application of these practices alone is not enough as a solution for the indicated problems. It is necessary to change the *culture* of the IT organization significantly, so that not only the tools, methods and techniques used evolve, but *the attitude of IT staff* to the key aspects of the company's work: customer's role, value created by information technology, tolerance to known shortcomings, and the need for continual improvement. Blind application of DevOps ideas: — for example, *"let's build a pipeline, because without it DevOps does not exist"* — is likely to lead to the phenomenon known as Cargo cult. This thesis will be discussed in more detail in Section 5.5 *Cargo culting*.

However, let us step back for a moment from these important matters and recall how DevOps originated.

1.4 The history of origination

It would seem that pragmatic consideration of a subject does not require immersion in its history: does it really matter, who met with whom and when, what was discussed and what they came up with?

If you approach DevOps as a set of techniques that you just need to 'implement' in your organization, then indeed you can skip this section. However, it appears that the success of DevOps transformation of any company directly depends on the people. It is the people that should change their practice of work. And it is the people that may not do this without adopting new values and understanding answers to the 'why?' and 'why now?' questions. So, let's spend a little time on a retrospective journey, since there are specific personalities behind all the events described below, with their past and current motivation.

As discussed in *Agile methods for software development,* by the second half of the 2000s, various techniques such as Agile, Scrum, XP, and the like have been widely adopted in the field of software development. Expanding them to the operations, most likely, was only a matter of time. One of the first documented attempts was made in 2006, when Marcel Wegermann published an article on the application of the principles of agile development to the work of system administrators[18]: he suggested to include separate system catalogues in the version control system; to use pair work of system administrators; to conduct operations retrospectives.

In 2008, at the regular conference on Agile held in Toronto, two significant events occurred at once. Andrew Shafer suggested including a new track 'Agile infrastructure' in the program, and Patrick Debois presented on 'Agile infrastructure and operations: how infra-gile are you?'[19] They had common interests in many respects, as A. Shafer just moved from development to operation, and P. Debois at that time worked simultaneously with developers and support, observing completely different approaches to work in each of the teams: since 2007, he was engaged in a large data centre migration project. According to his memoirs, the presentation did not make a big impression on the audience. Other participants of the conference said that the audience was also not big enough. However, further events showed that those who came, were very interested in the ideas outlined, and the ideas themselves were continued, and quite soon.

In the same 2008, Luke Kanies, founder of the Puppet Labs, spoke at an open source software conference on configuration management, which, in his opinion, needed to be reviewed. His report caught attention of John Willis, who later had a strong influence on the development of DevOps ideas. It is worth noting that the very term DevOps did not yet exist at that time.

The term DevOps was picked up after the presentation made by John Allspaw and Paul Hammond at the Velocity conference in 2009. The presentation entitled *10+ Deploys per Day: Dev and Ops Cooperation at Flickr*[20] made an indelible impression on many minds who were already interested in this topic in one way or another. P. Debois decided to organize the first specialized conference DevOpsDays, which was held in Ghent, Belgium, in the same year 2009[21]. In 2013 Gene Kim who attended the presentation, published *The Phoenix Project*[22] and founded the IT Revolution company, which promotes the subject and holds the DevOps Enterprise Summit[23] conference twice a year.

---

18 Davis, J. and K. Daniels, *Effective DevOps: Building a Culture of Collaboration, Affinity, and Tooling at Scale*, 2016, ISBN 9781491926437; Chapter 3. A History of Devops
19 http://www.jedi.be/presentations/IEEE-Agile-Infrastructure.pdf
20 http://velocityconf.com/velocity2009/public/schedule/detail/7641
21 https://legacy.devopsdays.org/events/2009-ghent/
22 Behr, K., G. Spafford, G. Kim, *The Phoenix Project: A Novel About IT, DevOps, and Helping Your Business Win*, 2013, ISBN 978-0988262508
23 https://events.itrevolution.com/

Thus, the term *DevOps* as well as the community of enthusiasts emerged...

> The *10+ deploys per day* presentation is currently considered the starting point of the DevOps movement.
>
> DevOpsDays is an extremely popular event in the life of the DevOps community, spanning many countries.
>
> DevOps Enterprise Summit is the largest and most representative DevOps conference, both in terms of the number of participants and the line-up of the speakers.
>
> *The Phoenix Project* book seems to be the best-selling book on DevOps in the world.
>
> Puppet Labs and IT Revolution companies are among the most prominent and influential players in the DevOps market.
>
> Most of the abovementioned personalities are considered absolute gurus among the DevOps illuminati of the world.

Looking back, one can make the following observations. First, the key ideas of DevOps emerged as a result of intellectual work seeking solutions to real management problems. Second, DevOps does not have one founding father or a group of fellows; the key people did always not know each other before, even if they had been thinking in similar directions. Third, DevOps does not and cannot have a copyright owner that dictates or defines development, or introduces restrictions on use (although some greedy commercial companies already reserve derivative trademarks, such as DevOps Foundation). Fourth, the DevOps subject is so new that it is too early to expect collections of proven recipes or universal methods to be available.

1.5   Frequently expressed misconceptions

The best way to complete this chapter is a review of common misconceptions. This will help to clearly establish the boundaries of the phenomenon and will allow us to proceed with more specific matters. The most complete coverage of all the misunderstandings encountered is not our objective; for this chapter, we selected those which help to understand *what* DevOps *is* from a management point of view, compared to *what* DevOps *is not*.

1.5.1   DevOps is a part of Agile

Fans of modern approaches to software development sometimes declare that DevOps is nothing more than the continuation of Agile ideas. At the heart of such a limited picture of the world lies the fact that agile development makes it possible to establish relationships with the customers in terms of understanding their requirements for the software product, and to release such software product quickly enough. The long-standing problem of "*What to do with a released product, to make it useful, and how to actually operate it*" now has a solution: DevOps! Someone will find answers to these awkward questions there.

For example, let's look at the popular SAFe (Scaled Agile Framework) model, designed to help with the application agile development to medium and large-scale organizations[24].

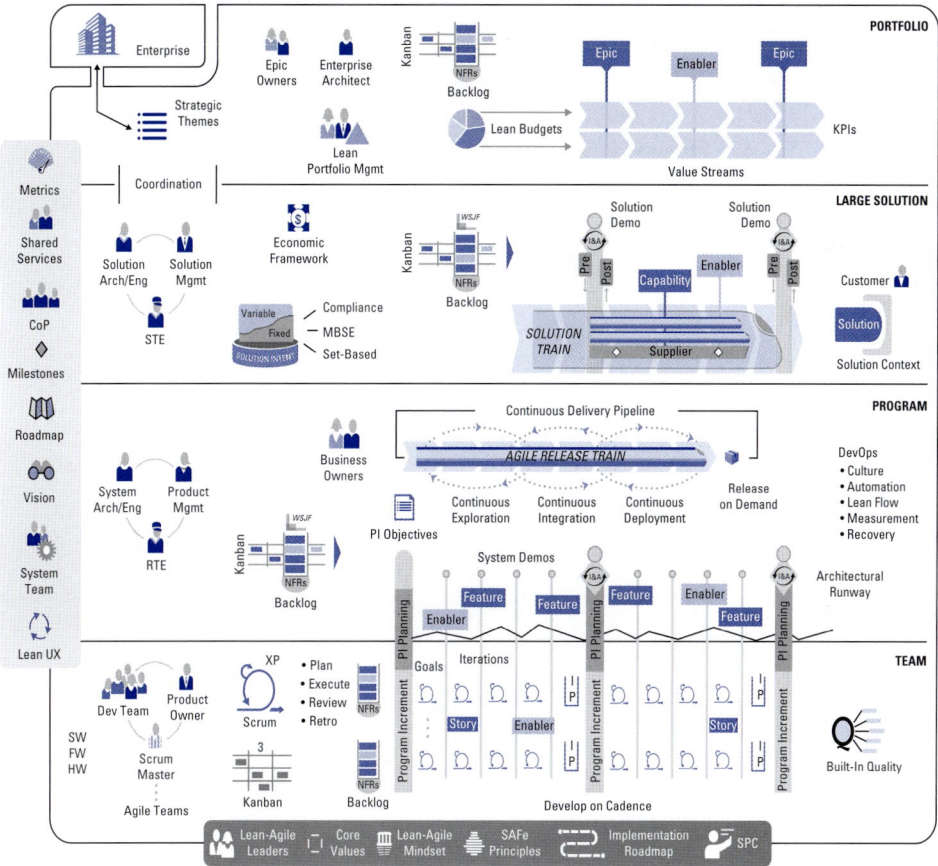

Fig. 1.11 SAFe model, version 4.6 (2018)

DevOps in question is on the right side of the model, approximately in the middle, in the 'Program' section. Judging by the font size, its significance roughly corresponds with those of 'Backlog', 'Kanban' and 'Business Owners'. Actually, the description of SAFe says[25]:

---

24 http://www.scaledagileframework.com/
25 http://www.scaledagileframework.com/devops/

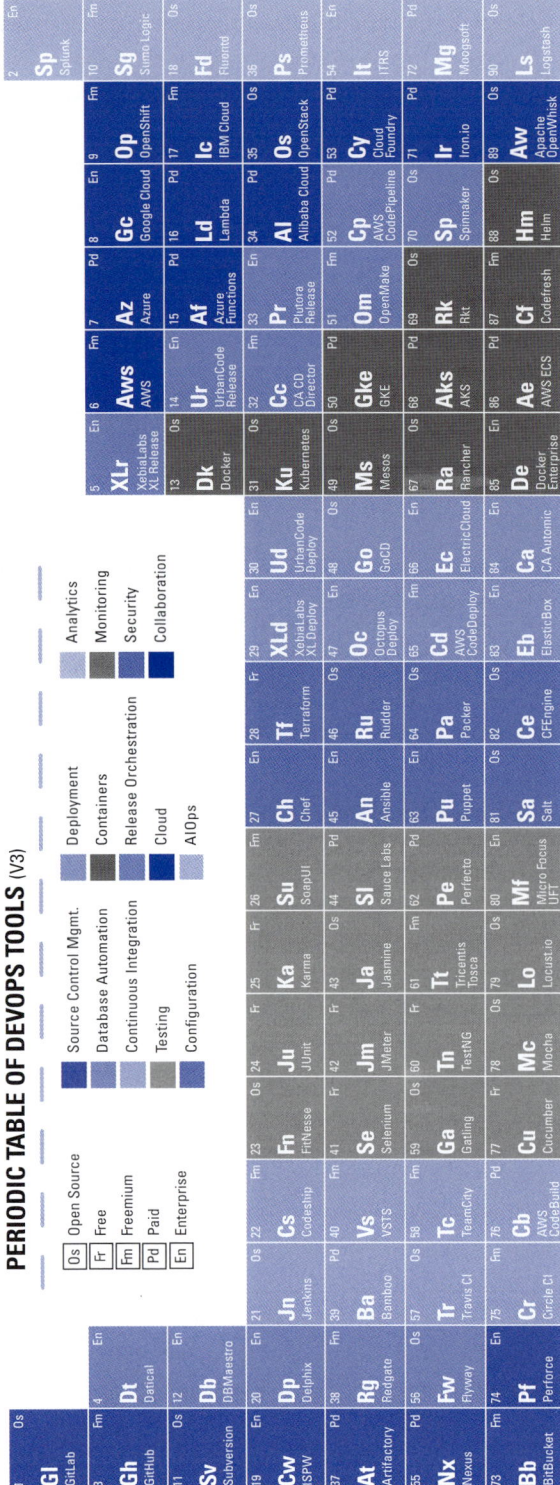

Fig. 1.12 'Periodic table' of DevOps tools by XebiaLabs, version[26]

[26] https://xebialabs.com/periodic-table-of-devops-tools/

SAFe enterprises implement DevOps to break down silos and empower each Agile Release Train (ART) and Solution Train to continuously deliver new Features to their end users. Over time, the separation between development and operations is significantly reduced... The goal is simple: Deliver value more frequently.

This is definitely a very limited view on DevOps, for at least three reasons. First, based largely on Agile, DevOps nevertheless extends the ideas of agile development to agile IT production in general, the whole organization, the whole process, the entire value chain (see *The Principles* below). Second, getting the return from DevOps requires more significant cultural changes in the company than it usually does for Agile (see Section 5.5 *Cargo culting*). Third, the objectives set for DevOps are not just limited to speeding up the delivery: there is also a need to reduce technical debt and to eliminate fragility (see Section 1.3 *Why DevOps?* above).

1.5.2   DevOps is all about tools and automation

"DevOps Conference for developers. World experts. Technical no-nonsense hardcore (18+)"

Advertisement in Google search,
October 2017

Another point of view is connected to the word *automation*. Software tools that help modern IT departments have multiplied in recent years; often there are hundreds of these. Many vendors will assure you that they *are* DevOps, or that their tools will provide you with the best DevOps tools.

The marketing pressure of vendors is very high. Large companies like CA, HP and Microsoft have already joined this club, bringing in their high revenue targets and proportionate marketing budgets. Many may notice a direct analogy to the history of twenty years ago, with the software for managing IT services: the software vendors also were saying then that ITSM was software and all you needed is to install it, and the processes would emerge by themselves. Only few vendors see and seriously discuss something outside the software.

DevOps indeed depends on the availability and effectiveness of certain automation tools. But strictly speaking, the minimum set of these tools can be reduced to a version control system for storing all source codes and IT infrastructure configuration data, and to software delivery pipeline automation system. Everything else, as they say, can be added to taste. While individual software solutions are widely adopted, there is no and cannot be a universal list of mandatory DevOps software. This book, in which one can study the phenomenon in detail without considering software products, without even mentioning their names at all, is the indirect confirmation that a particular implementation of DevOps can be software-independent.

1.5.3 DevOps is a new profession

The next option is suggested by recruitment agencies and job sites. They say that DevOps is a universal soldier, able to code, to create tests, to deploy environments, and to manage the infrastructure. That is, he or she can effectively perform the work of both the software developer and the support engineer, all for one salary.

Another common occurrence is the substitution of the famous ancient profession of system administrator to a more fashionable DevOps engineer. Looking at these vacancies, it is already clear from the description that they are not about DevOps at all.

> "A software startup is looking for a DevOps / System Administrator (Bitrix) to work remotely."
>
> Advertisement on the staff search site, October 2017

The third case is the DevOps guru, who is necessary for the 'implementation' of all this DevOps in a company. Similar to an Agile coach or a Scrum Master.

All these, of course, are serious misconceptions. DevOps is a profound change in the fundamentals of the IT department, which cannot be done by hiring a number of DevOps engineers or by inviting DevOps gurus. The ability to implement a software delivery pipeline does not guarantee success. It is unlikely to save costs by applying DevOps practices, as it was shown in the Section 1.3.1 *Decrease time to market*.

1.6 Summary

Let's conclude this chapter with a short summary of the main information that has been stated. For better understanding and for future references to the subject and communication with colleagues, it is presented in Figures 1.13 and 1.14 in graphic form.

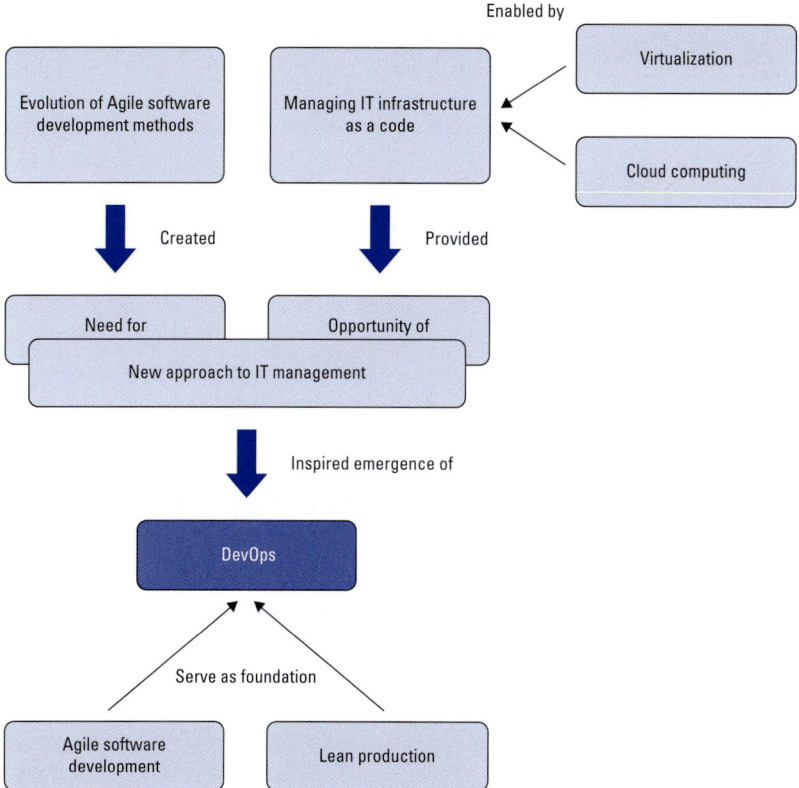

Fig. 1.13 DevOps' Picture of the World

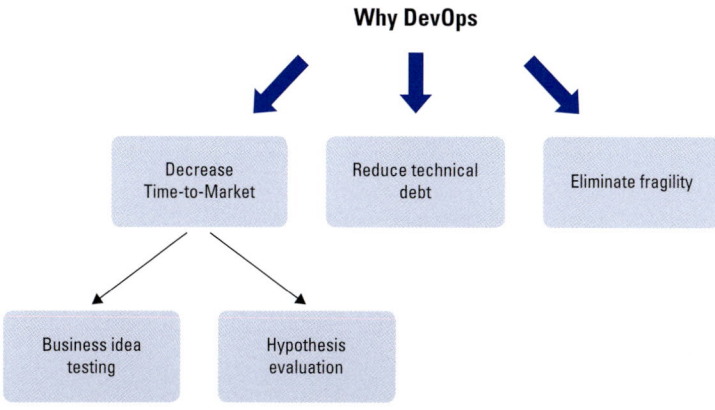

Fig. 1.14 Why DevOps

2 The Foundation

2.1 Lean production

2.1.1 Key facts

As mentioned in Section 1.2 *The definition*, DevOps relies heavily on the principles and practices of lean production. Some even believe that by and large there is nothing else in DevOps apart from these, but this is not true. To explain this, we need to consider the basics of lean production. It will give us a good idea of the foundation on which DevOps is built.

To put it simply, the idea of lean production may be reduced to identifying and eliminating waste. In order to better understand this statement, it is necessary to recall the problem that Lean initially tried to solve.

In the 1930s, a small company called Toyoda Automatic Loom Works, renamed later to Toyota, identified the opportunities in the car market development. On the one hand, the 'effective demand', i.e. the amount of money people were willing so spend on cars at that time was low, which meant that the product should be as cheap as possible. On the other hand, the size of the market was very modest, and it meant that it would not be possible to apply the principles of mass production and economies of scale. The company decided to find its own way, and further developments showed that it succeeded. The young engineer Taiichi Ohno (1912-1990) was employee at the Toyota works and the brain centre for the creation and development of the new production technology. He imagined the ideal picture: production begins only after the client has placed the order, and the new car is delivered to the client immediately. In order to achieve such production speed, it was necessary to perform only the operations that directly contribute to the product creation as soon as possible, while eliminating all potential waste.

In lean production, much attention is paid to the concept of waste: the usual, everyday meaning is supplemented and expanded in order to become an object of management in different areas of work. At the top level, the wastes are divided into *Muri*, *Mura* and *Muda*. *Muri* can be defined as a work of questionable value, which management assigns to employees due to non-optimal processes; utilization with constant overload or extra-high intensity. *Mura* means unevenness or inconsistency; it refers to uneven demand levels; scattering, fluctuations. *Muda* refers to wastes that occur during the work; their origins and properties are so unobvious that they require additional classification. The original list is given below; respective wastes in IT are taken from the publications of Mary Poppendieck and Tom Poppendieck[27]:

---

27 Poppendieck, M. and T. Poppendieck, *Lean Software Development: An Agile Toolkit*, 2003, ISBN 978-0321150783

Wastes	Explanation in terms of IT
Inventory Analogy of losses in IT: Partially done work	Unfinished work does not bring value to the end customer, while resources have already been used. The value realization of the unfinished work cannot be evaluated due to absence of feedback from the customer. The outputs of unfinished work done in order to exclude underutilization of the resources, may become obsolete, or not be required in the future.
Extra Processing Analogy of losses in IT: Extra processes	The extra processes are any steps of any process, except for analysis, programming, and deployment of the application. Including: documentation, coordination, planning, reporting and so on.
Overproduction Analogy of losses in IT: Extra features	Any extra features spend resources throughout the value chain: on analysis, coding, testing, deployment, operation. At the same time, a significant part of the functionality of a typical software is not used by clients, that is, it does not add value. Besides, extra features create additional potential failure points.
Transportation Analogy of losses in IT: Task switching	Task switching leads to time losses, including, among other things, focusing and immersion in the context. In general, the total time of doing several tasks simultaneously will be significantly higher than the total time spent on the same tasks done consecutively.
Waiting Analogy of losses in IT: Waiting	Waiting for something at any stage leads to delay of the entire value chain. Typical delays associated with waiting in IT are: waiting for a decision, waiting for the appointment or release of resources, waiting for the completion of documenting the previous steps, waiting for the organization's cycles (for example, budget, or other approval).
Motion Analogy of losses in IT: Handoffs	Obtaining the information required to complete the work may take considerable time or resources. Transfer of artifacts that occur at this stage can be done nonlinearly, as a complex process, and also require time or resources. For all this, physical movement of staff or documentation is often necessary.
Defects Analogy of losses in IT: Defects	Negative consequences of defects can be estimated as influence of these defects on the health of the IT system, taking into account the time during which the defect is present in the system. Even minor defects lead to serious losses over time.

Fig. 2.1 Types of manufacturing waste and their analogies in IT

As can be seen from the table above, almost all types of waste from the original list, taken from the field of lean production, are relevant for the field of information technology. Since the first information about Toyota's production system was published and the above basic ideas were understood, the extension of the original list was on the mind of many followers. Various authors proposed to add the following types of waste:

- management costs (essentially everything that is done by management, not workers);
- products or services that do not meet expectations and needs of customers (which resonates with the classical definition of the quality);
- unused creative and intellectual potential of employees;
- failure to use employees' resources to improve processes and technologies;
- insufficient staff training;
- using incorrect metrics, or not using measurements at all;
- inefficient use of information systems (low-quality automation, as well as waste from the unproductive use of information technology, such as: games and social networking during working hours).

Of course, with a bit of fantasy, the list of types of waste can be extended; just don't forget the basic principles of the waste concept, and remember the impact each waste type has on management decisions in practice. Speaking about the principles, the following one is the most common: waste is everything the clients would not pay for if they had a choice. Obviously, this statement is too generic and is hardly suitable for solving the problem of attributing a particular job as either value-creating or a waste, especially in borderline cases. For example, is a preliminary architecture planning of an IT system a waste? Is the integration testing of various source codes and modules a waste?

In my opinion, for practical application the basic principle can be formulated more precisely: wastes are the actions that are not necessary for obtaining the desired outcome; and that can be avoided or minimized by altering the process.

Practical application of lean production ideas can be described by the following sequence of steps:
1. Use specialized tools to *identify* waste;
2. Apply other specialized tools to *eliminate or reduce* waste;
3. Repeat step 1;
4. . . .
5. PROFIT!!!

Lean production uses many interesting concepts, practices and tools. DevOps borrows many of them, such as the value stream and value stream mapping; quick problem removal (Andon); steady and even flow; one task per unit of time; identifying and eliminating bottlenecks and constraints; continual improvement; pull system; work visualization and others. Some of them will be discussed in Chapters 3 *The Principles* and 4 *Key Practices*.

2.1.2 Challenges

Although the ideas of lean production are quite attractive, organizations that try to use these principles in their work, experience some difficulties. Even if one does not consider the application of Lean in the field of information technology, and looks at a broader experience in organizing production, one can see that the ideas of lean production may fail to have the expected effect. The main reason is a fairly substantial restructuring of the organization required: not only and not so much from the practices and tools perspective, but rather from the perspective of principles. These changes require a different corporate culture than the one that most organizations have. Employees must share common values, often different from those in 'traditional' companies. Let's have a look at an example: a worker walking along the shop notices some engine oil spilled on the floor next to one of the machines. In a company of the lean production spirit, the employee simply could not pass by — they must take action to eliminate the disorder, since they understand and share the view that the puddle may lead (and most likely will lead) to the production of poor-quality products, or a production slowdown. In a similar situation in an ordinary company, an employee is likely to simply pass by, because they are sure that this work is outside their duties, since there are specially trained people in the organization, whose responsibility is to keep things in order. It is clear that to cultivate a different, subtle culture across all members of staff is a complex, costly and long-term management task. Publications show that some organizations prove to be unable to solve it at all; in many cases the culture change takes years, if not decades.

> There is an interesting and well-known story of an attempt to spread the Toyota practices in a completely different environment, namely General Motors. In short, the events were as follows.
>
> Among all the GM car-manufacturing plants, the factory in Fremont, California, was the worst in terms of both product quality and management. The situation reached the point where employees openly drank and gambled in the workplace during their shifts, while managers could do nothing about it. In 1982, the plant was closed.
>
> Around the same time, Toyota tried to enter the US market, for which it needed to have a local production. The best solution seemed to be a partnership with an existing player: Toyota would get a quick start on the local market, and the partner would get access to Toyota technologies, including management techniques. In 1984, the same Fremont Assembly plant was reopened under the name of New United Motor Manufacturing, Inc. (NUMMI). Some employees, including former trade union leaders, kept their places. They were trained in Japan, and the management was enforced by valuable foreign personnel. Within a short time, the plant had become the best in GM in terms of both the product quality and its production culture. To say the least, the Japanese made a small miracle.
>
> Of course, a success story should be replicated. The next plant selected was Van Nuys, with similar problems to the one in Fremont. However, all attempts to change or improve anything totally failed, despite the involvement of experienced managers from the already successful NUMMI plant.
>
> *"You can see a lot of things different. But the one thing you don't see is the system that supports the NUMMI plant"*, GM managers recalled later. *"I don't think, at that time, anybody understood the large nature of this system. General Motors was a kind of throw it over the wall organization. The TPS exists — and can only succeed — within an ecosystem of organizational culture, supplier relations, financial management, HR, and governance designed around its philosophy..."*
>
> GM spent the next 15 years analysing the situation and deciding on the business case for changing the culture and production system. Another 10 years passed trying to implement the changes. In 2009, GM went bankrupt and was bought by the US government. In 2010, the NUMMI plant was closed, but Toyota remained in the North American market with a market share of about 15% in terms of the number of cars sold.

Those who try to apply Lean for the sake of Lean, and not in order to solve the existing problems, encounter similar difficulties. This practice can be found in many areas, we will not focus on it much. We will just note that, like other management principles and tools, lean production is a way of achieving goals that need to be defined beforehand, and then achieved with the given means.

The challenge of applying the lean production principles in the domain of information technology is that it's not easy to find any sort of a production pipeline in an ordinary IT department. At the same time, the practices used in Lean, such as Andon and just-in-time (JIT), are often associated with a pipeline. Indeed, if we consider the software development department as a separate, independent structure, then we can identify a pipeline related to the software life cycle. However, this pipeline does not end with provision of value to the end consumers (as it is limited to one of the IT teams), and is therefore incomplete. It is even harder to find a pipeline in IT Operations. Perhaps, that is the reason for some authors to present IT service delivery in a form of pipeline; the depth of this thought is hard to measure for anyone who is familiar with the basics of ITSM.

Very often, work of an IT department is intangible: it cannot be touched, or even seen, or evaluated. Exactly the same applies to the outputs: IT systems functioning or IT services being provided, depending on your point of view. The intangibility of *stock*, *labour* and *product* in IT is strikingly different from those at a production plant.

Let's complete reviewing the complexities of Lean application with a beautiful metaphor, suggested by the aforementioned Mary and Tom Poppendieck: if we take a restaurant as an example, creation of information systems is more like recipes made by the chef, and the production at the plant is closer to cooking meals by following the recipes developed earlier. The chef's work includes making a guess of the most elegant, delicious and demanded meals, finding the optimal way to produce them, testing this way, often in many cycles, by trial and error, and continual improvement of the menu. The production of the same dishes by the restaurant staff is closer to the pipeline, where products are cooked according to the provided recipe, including both the list of necessary ingredients and the cooking technology.

Thus, direct application of the principles and ideas of lean production is not always as simple as one would wish; especially if we consider the specifics of the modern IT.

2.2 Agile

2.2.1 Key facts

The origins, ideas and principles of Agile have been reviewed in the Section 1.1.1 *Agile methods for software development*. Agile serves as a strong foundation for DevOps; it is so strong, that you can even hear from time to time a bold statement made by some enthusiasts that there is nothing more than Agile in DevOps (let us recall the beginning of this chapter about lean production with a similar point). As with Lean, the story is similar with Agile: this statement is far from the truth.

It should be noted that Agile is originally a set of principles and values. Practical application of these principles, based on these values, is guided by derivative products — a variety of software development methods. There is at least a dozen of them available now, and the best known one is Scrum.

Without going into the details of different sources of knowledge and not aiming to investigate their origins, we can highlight those key ideas and practices of Agile, that are most often mentioned in DevOps:
- Forming of small independent and self-sufficient teams (up to 10-12 people), preferably co-located and focused on a limited scope;
- Sprint-based iterative process of creating and testing the program code with the delivery of a viable product with each iteration (sprint);
- Maintaining a list of functional and non-functional requirements (backlog), which serves as the input for planning of the next iteration;
- Splitting of the large tasks into small parts (stories), their evaluation in conventional workload units for prioritization;
- Active involvement of the customer representatives;
- Regular short stand-up meetings of the team to discuss the planned tasks, progress and present difficulties;
- Regular retrospectives helping the team to self-train and improve its work.

Some items on this list are discussed in more detail in Chapter 4 *Key Practices*.

2.2.2 Challenges
Despite the hype around Agile at this moment, the application of agile approach to software development faces difficulties in many cases.

First, as shown in the Section 1.1.1 *Agile methods for software development*, Agile covers only a part of the value chain, which leads to a modest overall effect.

Second, agile *development* methods do not take into account the specifics and complexity of the *operation* of information technologies, where iterative approach is less applicable, at least if applied bluntly.

Third, if, according to Scrum, the final output of the team's work at every iteration is merely a new code that has passed regression testing, the team's work will be reduced to a constant sprinting, day after day, week after week, and the staff will get less and less moral satisfaction from the work. Indeed, only team members can evaluate the elegance of the applied algorithms, while the developed software is operated by another team following different rules. Some companies report the burnout of their employees after a few dozen iterations.

Note that the history of Agile is far from complete, this area continues to develop. It is also notable that the key persons realize the complexity of the current moment: ten years after the publication of the Manifesto, they gathered again to discuss achievements and problems. One of the outputs of the meeting was a list of 20 problems of the movement, which are not really meant to be discussed publicly[28]. The following are among them: the direct commercial interest of many founders censoring failures; pretending Agile is not a business; hushing up the difficulties and negative cases; failure to describe the context in which some practices work, or do not work, and constant return to dogmas, bigotry, and claims of universal applicability; blurred and unproven business value proposition; scaling naïveté; increase and accumulation of technical debt.

All this does not mean that Agile should be written off. On the contrary, these are all reasons to use practical know-how, in order to move further from this platform into DevOps.

> It is interesting to read how Philippe Kruchten, who attended the memorable meeting dedicated to the anniversary of Agile in 2011, summed up the first years of the idea's existence:
>
> *The agile movement is in some ways a bit like a teenager: very self-conscious, checking constantly its appearance in a mirror, accepting few criticisms, only interested in being with its peers, rejecting en bloc all wisdom from the past, just because it is from the past, adopting fads and new jargon, at times cocky and arrogant. But I have no doubts that it will mature further, become more open to the outside world, more reflective, and also therefore more effective.*

---

28 https://www.infoq.com/articles/agile-teenage-crisis

3 The Principles

It is useful to separate principles from practices. Of course, each of these two words can have different meanings, so we need to agree on the definitions first. By principles we mean the key ideas on which DevOps is based; if they are not adopted and applied, DevOps makes a very little sense. By practices we mean activities performed in accordance with principles to produce a desired outcome. The principles stay unchanged for any organization that applies DevOps, while the practices will most likely be adopted and adapted depending on the specific context.

> As to methods, there may be a million and then some, but principles are few. The man who grasps principles can successfully select his own methods. The man who tries methods, ignoring principles, is sure to have trouble.[29]
>
> Harrington Emerson, American engineer and business theorist, pioneer of the scientific management discipline, 1911

The core principles described by international DevOps experts are given in this chapter. In Chapter 4 we will discuss the practices.

3.1 Value stream

One of the key concepts of DevOps, borrowed from lean production is the value stream. This concept has been used for a long time, but with the expansion of its practical application new publications appear that sufficiently cover the topic from a hands-on perspective[30].

It is useful to consider the work of an organization in terms of creating value in response to a consumer's request. The actions performed to fulfil the query are lined up in a sequence called value stream. Typically, an organization processes a variety of different requests. At the same time, a traditional organization works on several products or services. Thus, there are a lot of value streams in the company.

---

29 https://www.goodreads.com/quotes/346365-as-to-methods-there-may-be-a-million-and-then
30 We recommend the following:
- Rother, M. and J. Shook, *Learning to See: Value-Stream Mapping to Create Value and Eliminate Muda*, Lean Enterprise Institute, 2009, ISBN 978-0966784305
- Martin, K. and M. Osterling, *Value Stream Mapping: How to Visualize Work and Align Leadership for Organizational Transformation*, McGraw-Hill, 2014, ISBN 978-0071828918

Work on the stream visualization is known as value stream mapping. It starts with the selection of a product: sometimes, the one with the greatest opportunities for optimization; sometimes the one promising the quickest significant improvements, at the same time providing material to study the method. Mapping is done in two steps: first, the as-is picture is created, then the to-be one. The study of the to-be map is important for two reasons. First, it helps to avoid local optimization, which will be discussed a little later. Second, understanding of the target state allows to launch a realistic improvement mechanism, with a clear (as clear as possible) direction of improvement.

Actually, the value stream mapping exercise is simple: you need to identify the key steps of the request processing, to document the work performed at each of them, to arrange these steps into a sequence of creation of the desired outcome. One of the difficulties is the excessive level of details, when the resulting map does not fit on one sheet. The authors of the abovementioned books recommend to limit the number of map blocks to fifteen; to make further work with the map easier. The second difficulty is to agree about what the exact steps are, how and by whom they are carried out. In some organizations, there is no common understanding of the process, which leads to many hours of disputes.

Once the map is built, it can be filled with further important details. It may be useful to add the names of the responsible roles or people. It is also a good idea to specify the steps where the queues awaiting processing are accumulated; or the steps where delays occur due to waiting for a scheduled event — for example, a monthly CAB meeting or a quarterly budget review. Finally, the most valuable information is the three metrics for each step of the flow, namely Lead Time (LT), Process Time (PT), and the Percent Complete and Accurate (%C/A). Calculation of the values of these metrics in practice is a great challenge for an organization that is not equipped with relevant tools and practices. The employees performing the stream mapping, tend to underestimate the LT and PT indicators. Sometimes, on the contrary, people appeal to extreme cases where requests have been processed for too long, thus trying to overestimate the lead time. The situation with the %C/A metric is even worse, since its value for each step is usually unknown, and can only be guessed. It is important to remember that to map the stream 'as is', it is necessary to study actual practice, rather than its version documented in various guidelines, existing in the fantasies of the managers or applicable only in rare exceptional cases.

An example of a value stream map is given below.

Why do we need value stream mapping and why is this stream concept so important for DevOps? First, the very exercise of creating a map and understanding the as-is values of the key metrics has a sobering effect on the participants of the process. Usually, many understand that current practice has some points of inefficiency, but no one knows the scale of the disaster, especially in numbers. In the above example, the ratio of productive

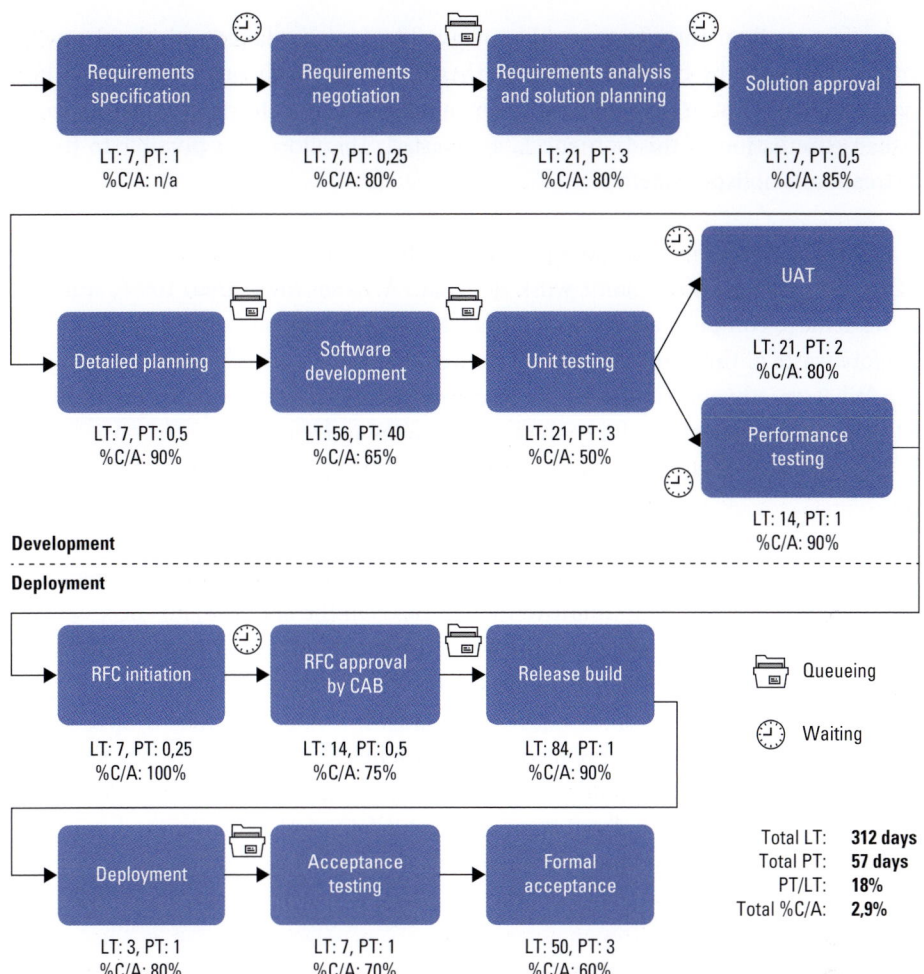

Fig. 3.1 Example of a value stream map

time spent on creating the desired outcome (value creation) is only 18% of the total time spent. This value in the example is given not far from reality; similar numbers are typical in average IT departments. The situation is even worse with the %C/A indicator, if the organization has a habit of returning to the previous steps tasks that were found to be incomplete or deviating from the assignment.

Second, a visual representation of the process helps to focus on the created value, rather than on the actions being performed. Usually employees and managers tend to see and understand their daily tasks (the 'what' of their work) quite well, while missing the expected outcome (the 'why').

Third, the value stream map helps to identify and eliminate bottlenecks, while avoiding the local optimization trap: time and effort spent to eliminate constraints that would not give effect at all, or the effect would be negligible. In accordance with the theory of constraints, proposed by Eliyahu Goldratt[31], there is one and only one real bottleneck in any system at one point in time, that slows down the work, and efforts spent on anything other than elimination of this bottleneck, are wasted. Therefore, it is possible to treat a value stream as a holistic system.

There are several questions that usually arise after the stream mapping:
1. [%C/A]: Why demonstrate some work steps %C/A values lower than 100%, and how can we achieve complete absence of errors transferred from one step to another (and therefore waste of time and resources for reworking)?
2. [LT]: What exactly contributes to the lead time, apart from creation of the product, and how can we radically reduce time lost in queues and waiting?
3. [PT]: How can we change the working practices, to reduce the processing time at each step?

It is worth noting that this optimization work should not be limited solely to analyzing the as-is map and attempting to improve the metrics. On the contrary, it is necessary to develop a to-be map, which may be quite different from the current work practice. This is exactly where DevOps tools and practices may help you to change the way your IT works.

And, finally, the fourth, awareness of the value stream helps to realize one of the key ideas of DevOps: a smooth and uniform flow from step to step that allows to deliver outputs continuously, rhythmically, without unnecessary delays and with optimal resource utilization.

3.2   Deployment pipeline

Understanding the value stream is a necessary and important step on the way to DevOps. However, working with the stream 'on paper' is not sufficient. The factors described in Section 1.1 *Origins* allow taking the next important step: to build a deployment pipeline. The need to build something like a pipeline is clearly illustrated by the following example: try noting the time that is required for a new line of code in any of your applications to take effect in the production environment. If the result is measured in days, weeks or months, your value stream needs to be seriously revised. The deployment pipeline is called to help this revision, meaning the most automated transition of changes through all steps of the value stream, starting from the 'Development is complete' point, down to 'Deployed into operations'.

---

31   https://www.tocinstitute.org/theory-of-constraints.html

The deployment pipeline operation can be illustrated by the following scheme:

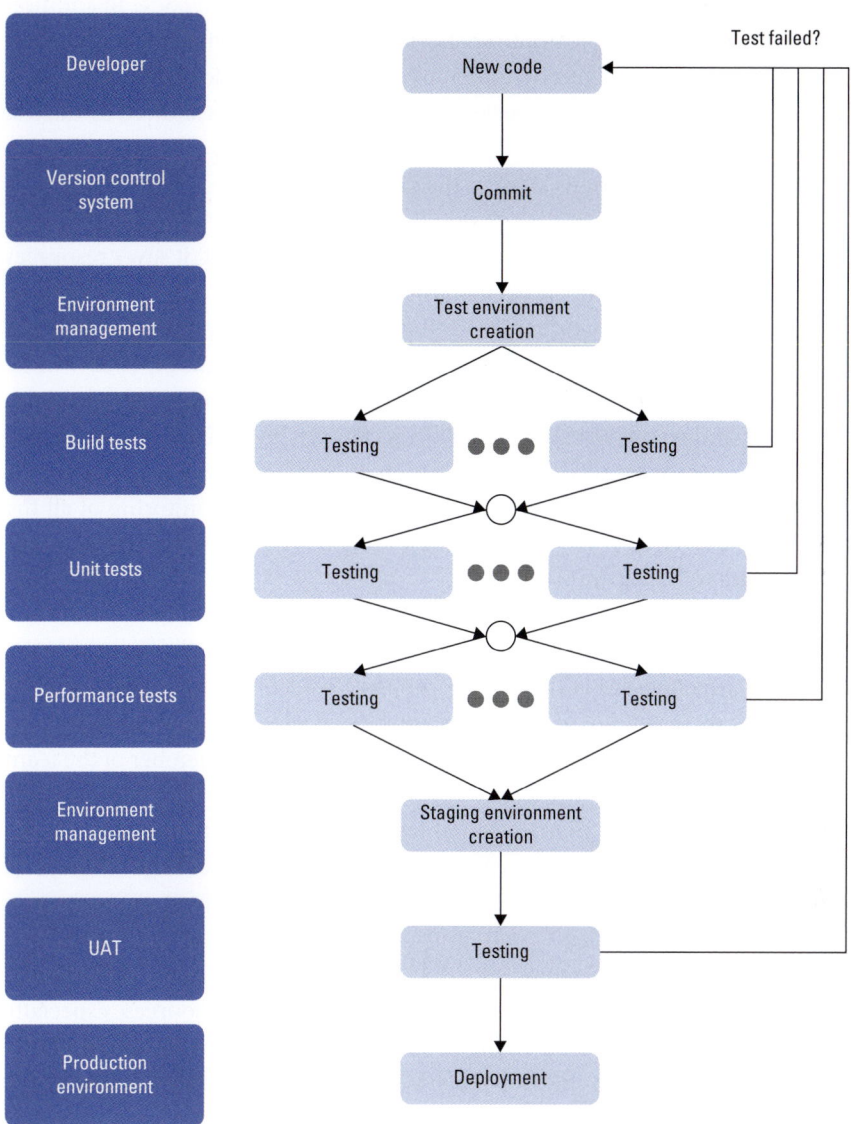

Fig. 3.2   Deployment pipeline

The pipeline automatically starts after the developer places a new piece of code in the version control system; at the same time the information about the change is recorded: who made the change, when was it made and what was changed? In response to the new record, the required temporary test environment is automatically created, where the pre-developed tests are started in sequence. The test sequence logic is simple: tests that detect the majority of errors are located at the beginning of the pipeline. All tests that require manual work (if any) are placed at the end of the pipeline. Failure to pass any of the tests results in providing the feedback to the developer and interruption of the pipeline for this change. To start the pipeline again, the developer must fix the program code. In addition to the test environment, it is possible to automatically create other environments required for the pipeline. The resources taken by these environments are automatically released after use. Of course, parallel execution of several tests is possible, if it is allowed by the test logic and if it does not introduce unproductive utilization of resources for testing changes that could be declined at the previous steps of the pipeline.

So, the pipeline helps to deal with three important DevOps tasks. First, it saves resources by not starting the next steps before the previous ones are complete. Second, the pipeline ensures the quality of the product — changes failing to perform as required, do not reach production environment, and the system is always in working condition (this will be covered later). Quality here means all the aspects related to functionality, performance, availability, security, and so on. Third, the pipeline accelerates the delivery of changes to the production environment by maximizing the automation of each step. And fourth, the pipeline constantly leaves records in the audit logs, which enables monitoring of all the changes being made, as well as accurate measurements at all steps of the pipeline, which provides valuable data for its optimization.

Implementation of a deployment pipeline introduces the following challenges:
1. Excessive enthusiasm for automation at the expense of ideology (processes, people, and culture) leads to creation of remarkably automated pipelines that nobody uses. The solution is obvious: DevOps is not just automation, and every member of the team should understand this.
2. Initially, there are not enough pre-developed tests to ensure steady operation of the pipeline. There is no other solution for this problem than to increase the coverage of the code with tests: the accumulated technical debt is due to be paid out sooner or later.
3. In the target state, there are so many tests that the passage of a change through the pipeline takes too long and requires significant computational resources, especially in case of a large amount of small changes. Companies experiencing this problem actively use the so-called Test Impact Analysis. Under this slightly incorrect, but already established name, it is a practice where, using special marks and artificial intelligence tools, the testing system selects from the variety of tests those that relate to the proposed change, without performing the remaining tests.

> Many believe that the name 'pipeline' is taken by analogy with an assembly line, for example, in a car manufacturing plant. Others believe that the word 'pipeline refers to a liquid or other substance flowing through the pipes, and the deployment pipeline should follow this analogy. Both above opinions are inaccurate.

> As the authors of the term, Jez Humble and David Farley[32], explain, the idea originated from the pipelining used in modern processors, where performance improvements cannot be achieved solely by increasing the clock frequency. The architectural solution used is the parallel execution of instructions, which initially come in sequence. To do this, the processor must 'guess' the results of processing in a parallel flow, 'assuming' that they will be as required to perform calculations in the current flow. If not, the results of the calculations will be discarded. The time lost due to this 'unlucky guess' is more than compensated by the acceleration for those cases when the 'guess' was correct.
>
> So, a properly implemented deployment pipeline allows to make development and testing independent of each other in time: it is assumed that testing will be successful, so you can proceed to the next batch of work. The same logic is applied to the parallel testing.

There are three more concepts important for DevOps that are related to deployment pipeline: continuous integration, continuous delivery and continuous deployment. Their interpretations vary; the following description is based on opinion of the experts these concepts originate from.

It is customary to understand *continuous integration* as the process of the constant assembly of program code; *continuous* means every time a developer places a change in the version control system. The usual practice of software development involves many separate branches of code, where different programmers and teams work for a long time (days, weeks and months) to create new functionality. At the end of each part of the development, or, even worse, after waiting for all teams working on one product to complete their development, a painful process of assembling all the changes into a single build begins. Since there are a lot of programmers, who generally work asynchronously, each of them works on a large change and for a long time, the assembly process itself becomes a time-consuming task, which may take several weeks. Indeed, it is important to take into account all the changes, compare them with each other, update the tests by factoring in the changes and comparisons, rewrite some or all of the earlier developed functionality, and repeat all this until the new code is brought to operational state. Assembly is an important stage in software development, and, in fact, the first test. Further work heavily depends on the assembly success.

Continuous integration, first described in 1999 in Ken Beck's book *Extreme Programming Explained*, proposes to simplify the assembly and to turn it into a routine. It is expected that programmers will work in the minimum number of branches, ideally in a common unified code base. It is also assumed that developers make minimal changes, portioned, each of which carries a small risk, but immediately starts the assembly process; so, each

---

[32] Humble, J. and D. Farley, *Continuous Delivery: Reliable Software Releases through Build, Test and Deployment Automation*, 2010, ISBN 978-0321601919

programmer places his code in the version control system at least once a day. Initial testing, performed automatically at each assembly, allows to immediately identify and correct errors, which means that the system is always maintained in working state.

Continuous delivery, described in detail in 2010 by Jez Humble and David Farley in the book of the same name, expands the idea of continuous integration: every saving of the changed code in the version control system triggers the assembly process and the entire deployment pipeline. Therefore, all changes that were not fully and successfully tested are not accepted and require immediate correction. And all error-free changes move the system to the state of full readiness for deployment in the production environment.

Continuous deployment means transition from the state *the system is always ready to deploy, with all the changes made* to the state *every change is immediately deployed in the production environment*. This transition requires redefining the *release* term: it's not IT anymore, but the business decides when certain new functionality will be available. Technically, it is already present in the production environment, immediately after completion of development and testing, but its activation can be performed additionally via program settings, when it is required, say, by the marketing department. This practice is known as Shadow Release or Dark Launches.

In any case, all these practices are based on the same deployment pipeline principle described above.

3.3 Everything should be stored in a version control system

Modern software developers are accustomed to version control systems. The first tools of this kind, called the source code storage systems, emerged in the 1970s. Nowadays it is hard to find a programmer who is not familiar with Git, Subversion or Mercurial. And not just the programmers: also many web masters use these systems for storing not only the source code, but also copies of the production environment, for example, for interpreted Internet systems or websites.

DevOps expands the use of such systems, like it does in many other areas. It's about storing not only the source code, but absolutely everything related to the IT system: tests, scripts for creating and modifying databases, build scripts, environment creation scripts (including the development environment), deployment scripts, artifacts, libraries, documentation, configuration files, even development tools, such as compilers, IDE, etc. It would be appropriate to put additional 'all' before each element of the above list: all tests, all scripts and so on. The only exception is for binary code after the compilation, for it usually takes up a significant space (especially if recreated after each change) and can be reproduced if everything else is in the storage system.

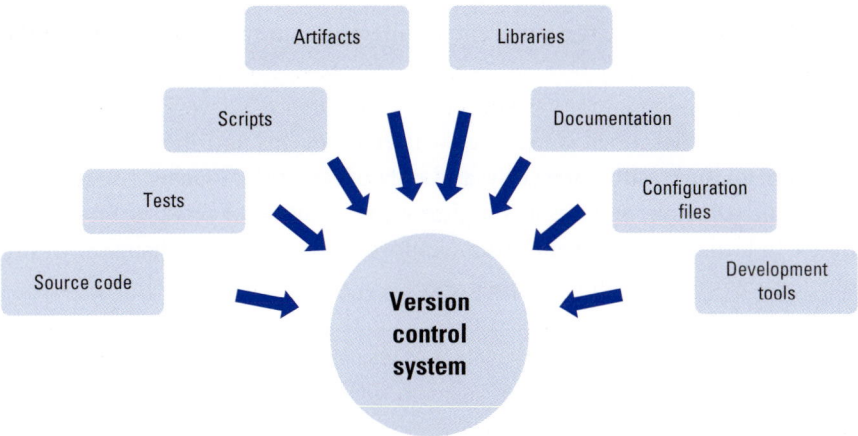

Fig. 3.3   Version control system

This principle allows for an unprecedented level of control over all the constituent parts of the system in operation, unattainable with other tools. Of course, the application of this principle requires a change in the culture of working with information and configurations.

One consequence is the ability to determine what was changed, when and by whom. Another important feature is the ability to restore the system as at any point in the past, including a return of the failed system in a guaranteed working state with minimal efforts. Another emerging feature, albeit less significant, is allowing any member of the team to freely delete unnecessary files and documents, without the risk of accidental loss of important information or product. It is known that as the product develops, the number of accompanying files increases, as well as the number of changes introduced. Cleaning up the debris is risky, unless there is a continuously created controlled copy.

3.4   Automated configuration management

Further developing the principle described above, DevOps completely restructures the management of the production environment (as well as any other environments). The traditional practice of many organizations is as follows: a new server is created from a pre-defined image, then the administrator manually sets it up it, installing and configuring additional software packages, both system and application. If it is necessary to change the set of packages or their configurations, the administrator connects to the server under his account and manually makes the necessary settings.

This practice is completely impossible in the DevOps world: any changes to any environment can be made only by scripts stored in the version control system. For example, if you need to have a new library in the test environment tomorrow, the administrator should update the script for creating the test environment, test it and place it in the version control system. Creation of environments is done automatically when the deployment pipeline is running.

Many of the previously described differences between DevOps and the usual practice affected development and testing primarily, and only occasionally touched the interests of operations. This principle requires a complete reorganization of work of IT support and operations. Indeed, at this moment administrators have no rights to change anything in the production environment in their usual ways.

> It is a common misconception that the complete DevOps sets in when developers get administrator's rights in the production environment, which blurs the responsibility and undermines the reliability of the system.
>
> In fact, it can be argued that even administrators are now deprived of their rights in the production environment, since from now on they are not allowed to change anything other than through fully controlled scripts.

DevOps configuration management provides the same benefits that are obtained from the total version control, but now the primary beneficiaries are people working in Operations. Now all changes are controlled, the system can be quickly restored to the stable state; if the key members leave, the knowledge is not lost, and so on.

Some DevOps devotees defend this practice so zealously that they suggest use of a total IT infrastructure audit system to detect any unauthorized changes on any site, followed by immediate dismissal of the employee who has managed to manually configure a server or a network element. For small and medium-sized companies, this practice may seem excessive, but if you have thousands of servers and hundreds of engineers, then there might be no other way to ensure sustainability, quality and speed.

Some teams go to even further: administrators' passwords for various environments are regularly and automatically changed, without reporting new passwords to the IT staff. This prevents a production environment from unauthorized changes; although, this practice applies to all environments: development, test, and others.

3.5 The Definition of Done

The traditional attitude of an average employee to the work can be roughly defined by the phrase: *I did my job, I'm done*. Indeed, people are paid for what they do. The analyst defined functional requirements— their work is completed. The developer wrote the program code— they fulfilled their part of the overall business. The testers did the testing— they completed their part, and so on. However, everything is completely different in DevOps.

One of the key principles is: it is not when someone did their part of the work that it is done, but when the customer received or started to receive the value they expected. This means that the entire value stream has been followed through completely up to the production environment; only then the work will be considered done.

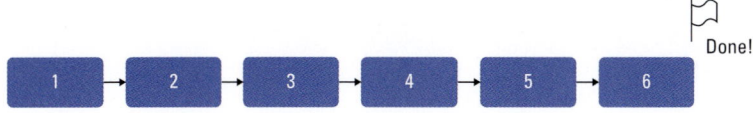

Fig. 3.4   Definition of Done

Though this principle seems obvious, following it does not happen organically and requires managerial efforts. Due to these efforts, the following benefits can be obtained:
1. The team focuses not on doing the work (*what* we do), but on the results, the value for the client (*why* we do it).
2. Limited responsibility for certain areas of work (*"no complaints about the buttons?"*) is washed off, replaced by a collective responsibility for the overall result of the team (*"the suit must fit"*).

Radically-minded DevOps devotees insist on a more rigid Definition of Done. They suggest the approach where creation of new functionality is done only when the application is running in the production environment and all the assembly, testing and deployment activities are done automatically.

3.6   Summary

To summarize this chapter, let's recall the definition of principles given at the beginning. It says, *principles are the key ideas on which DevOps is based; if they are not adopted and applied, DevOps makes a very little sense.*

Indeed, without understanding, accepting and using value stream, deployment pipeline, full version control system, automated configuration management, and the Definition of Done, one can play with DevOps practices for as long as one likes, but the outcome will never be significant.

4 Key Practices

4.1 Key differences from traditional practices

In the previous chapters of the book, we discussed the background and origins of DevOps, its foundation, its relationship to agile development and lean production, and important principles that make DevOps possible. By this point, a watchful reader of the book who's profession is a well-defined area (such as programming, analysis, architecture) probably would have already formed an understanding of what the subject is, why and who needs it, and what it includes. Unfortunately, with publications on IT management, be it ITIL®, COBIT or DevOps, this will not pass. The reader is likely to understand all the lofty matters described above, but they really want to get the answers to the specific questions: what is DevOps in practice? What exactly should be done and how?

Fortunately, there is a wonderful approach, which clearly illustrates the essence of the phenomenon through comparison with conventional 'traditional' practices: highlighting the differences will help to catch the most important. I used this approach in the training courses, workshops and business simulations on DevOps, conducted by Cleverics; this experience helps me to make the comparison as concise as possible, discarding unnecessary details, and selecting the most vivid examples.

4.1.1 Release is a routine

Every release is a great challenge in the daily work of an IT department. As a rule, a release includes several changes addressing several customers' requests. In addition, changes initiated by the IT department, are normally added to the release: those needed to keep the systems up and running or to improve performance (making systems more stable, safer, faster, and so on). To test and validate such a big release is a task in itself; it requires attention and time; it takes a lot of resources. Everyone knows that for any given release something will inevitably go wrong, and because of that the IT specialists:

- document all changes (in fact, not all of them);
- ensure that backups are made (for large systems it requires a lot of space and time, creating additional load on systems and networks, and still someone will forget to backup some important files);
- plan special actions and develop step-by-step instructions on returning the system, if possible, to the original state when something goes wrong (it is especially interesting in the cases where release is partially installed and partially not);
- plan releases in accordance with the agreed change schedule; use pre-agreed release windows to stop the systems if everything goes well, or in emergency, if something goes wrong (usually release windows fall on the long night from Friday to Monday);

- finally, deploy the release, while doing a fairly large number of operations manually (and not recording intermediate results).

Depending on how thoroughly each of the items on this list is worked through, the duration of the entire deployment can vary from a few days to several weeks. The number of the administrators' and developers' sleepless nights depends on the size of the release, the state of the IT system and efforts required to prepare and distribute the release.

In DevOps, a release is a routine. Releases are done weekly, and even daily. Of course, it requires a drastic reduction of the size of the introduced changes, but not only this: it is also necessary to radically revise the practice of preparing and distributing releases... Let's recall the pipeline and the practices of continuous integration and continuous delivery: they allow to document all the changes in the version control system, to perform most operations with automated tools, to log all the changes, and to set up the monitoring of new and changed components immediately after deployment. In case of any problems with the deployment, the pipeline will automatically stop it, roll back the changes already made and notify the team to take action.

For at least four years, the Puppet company together with several other organizations, has been preparing and releasing the annual State of DevOps report[33]. The 2017 report is based on input from about 3,000 respondents from different companies in different economic sectors; in total, more than 27,000 people were surveyed over the years. The authors of the report roughly divide all respondents into three groups: IT teams of high, medium and low productivity. The best way the *release is a routine* thesis can be illustrated is by the difference in the frequency of deployments: for low-productivity IT teams, the median frequency is in the range from weekly to monthly, while high-performance teams make several deployments a day.

4.1.2 Release is a business decision

Strictly speaking, the term *release* is not entirely correctly used in the previous paragraphs. The thing is that a release in ITSM and a release in DevOps have different definitions. For classic IT management (is it really possible to call ITSM classic IT management?), a release is a group of changes jointly deployed to the production environment. A release in DevOps means making a new functionality fully or partially available to users. To be precise, we should have used the word *deployment* instead of *release* for DevOps in Chapter 3.

In usual practice, a release is an IT decision. There is a release policy, and a release schedule, that defines release frequency and scale, and even the rules for version naming and numbering. The business unit in need for the new functionality gets in the queue

---

[33] https://puppet.com/resources/whitepaper/state-of-devops-report

and waits for release to follow: the next one (if they are lucky), but often — in one or two quarters.

When using continuous deployment in DevOps, the new functionality is deployed to the production environment as soon as it is developed and tested. Users do not notice it until it is activated. The activation is carried out when it is necessary for the business unit in accordance with its marketing, promotional or other plans and considerations. This practice was mentioned in the *Deployment pipeline* above; not only it allows to transfer release management into customer's hands, but also to gain additional benefits.

First, the downtime during releases is drastically reduced, down to zero (hence, *Zero-Downtime Releases*). Second, it becomes possible to perform so-called Blue-Green Deployments, where two copies of the production environment are created: 'green' and 'blue' respectively. Switching users from one environment where they are still interacting with the previous version of the application, to another where the new version is already running, is a matter of less than a second. Third, companies with a large number of users can use the technique of so-called Canary[34] Releases, when the new functionality first becomes available to a small number of users. After ensuring that everything is in order from the technical and marketing points of view, the decision to switch all other users to the new version can be made. The initial segmentation is performed by business units according to the logic that is important and familiar to them: depending on location, tariff plans, customer loyalty, and others. And fourth, many companies begin to actively apply A/B testing to test business hypotheses when some users (reference group) work with the old version of the system, and the other part (the experimental group) uses a new version. Comparison of the key groups' metrics allows to test and validate business ideas and to adjust further development of the system.

> One Facebook engineer was once asked: what is the probability that a particular Facebook user is participating in some experiment without knowing it? The engineer replied:
>
> *"Definitely 100%. We carry out more than twenty experiments constantly and simultaneously".*

All of the above becomes possible only if the very definition of release is changed and the decision is transferred to the business.

---

34 For several centuries miners took to the mine a cage with a canary: this bird is very sensitive to methane and carbon monoxide, and it dies even when their concentration in the air is insignificant, which was a signal for the miners to leave the mine immediately and return to the surface.

4.1.3 Everything is automated

If applied to IT, the famous (in Russia) proverb *"Laziness is the mother of invention"* can be transformed into *"A lazy administrator will eventually write a script to work less"*. In the traditional IT department, one can spend a long time waiting for the scripts to be written, there is no single repository, their performance is still in question, so most operations are done manually, even the ones that are often repeated. Examples of these operations:
- creating environments (testing, intermediate and others);
- configuration of the infrastructure components;
- testing;
- deployment and distribution, including the configuration of monitoring tools.

Increase of the level of control is crucial for DevOps, as described earlier in Section 3.3 *Everything should be stored in a version control system*. It requires total automation of all manual operations, especially those listed above.

The environments required for the deployment pipeline are created by scripts automatically, under control of the pipeline control system. Also, these environments are automatically decommissioned after use, freeing up resources. The configuration of IT infrastructure elements was discussed in detail in Section 3.4 *Automated configuration management*. Fast operation of the pipeline requires maximum possible automation of testing. Manual testing remains the last resort, although new solutions constantly shift this boundary: today you can perform automated testing of not only components, integration, regression, functionality, performance, but also of user interface, usability, and acceptance testing. Deployment and distribution, the final steps of the pipeline, are also done automatically, with the necessary adjustment to the systems and applications monitoring. The latter cannot be underestimated: quality monitoring allows getting very quick feedback on new releases. No matter how we try to make the test environment production-like, the difference still may show after the deployment. In this case an event recorded by the monitoring system can lead to an automatic rollback of the deployed change to ensure stability of the environment and applications.

Moreover, in the transition from traditional monolithic architectures to microservices, full monitoring of components becomes an urgent necessity: this is the only way to track not only the availability, but also the actual use of a particular service or service version by other services. Without this control, the evolving architecture will not be able to develop and it will permanently accumulate services that are already dead, but still connected (more details will be discussed in Section 5.3 *Evolving architecture*).

4.1.4 Incidents are solved immediately

A typical process for managing service incidents, when a user reports a failure, is as follows:

- a user contacts the first line of support via telephone, e-mail, portal, online chat or mobile application;
- the first line (with some help from the user, an automated system or artificial intelligence) logs and classifies the call, which often includes prioritization to set up the speed of further processing;
- the call gets in the queue, where it waits for its turn to come soon, or sometimes not so soon.

Processing of the infrastructure incidents, when system failure is reported by an IT specialist or a monitoring system, is structured roughly the same way, ending with a queue. The queue is an important control mechanism, helping to put the support tasks in order, and to load resources more evenly. It is also necessary because incident resolution normally takes a significant time. Each incident requires investigation, diagnostics, identification and implementation of a workaround — and in the vast majority of cases all this is done manually.

It's not like that in DevOps. In case the incident is traced back to a recent deployment, the pipeline control system will automatically roll back to the previous known stable state. Human intervention is still required to analyze the change and correct it, but it is much easier and faster, because the change was made quite recently, not several months or years ago. All links of the chain are known: the problem to solve, the customer, the developer, the tester.

In the event when something 'broke' in the infrastructure, the usual decision is to disconnect the failed component (for example, the application server) without much investigation and to create this section of the infrastructure again, using those ready-to-use scripts that previously were used to create this component. This operation saves a lot of time, compared to the traditional process. Indeed, if there are several dozens of servers controlled by the IT department, one can manually configure each of them, make up unique and beautiful names, nourish and cherish them. But if the IT department manages hundreds and thousands of servers, this introduces too many constraints and is no longer a productive way. The DevOps alternative is often called *Cattle versus Pets*. Let's recall that DevOps implies maximum abstraction from the physical hardware in favour of virtualization, as described in Section 1.1.2 *Managing infrastructure as code*.

4.1.5 Defects are fixed immediately

In the work of a typical IT department, defects that managed to pass through testing, and have been identified during operations, are evaluated, prioritized and queued up. There is nothing wrong with this approach, except for the fact that many of the errors stay in the queue forever, thus accumulating technical debt. Assigning a minor priority, the team postpones fixing of such errors for a long time. By then, everyone will have long forgotten what kind of defect it was, why it had occurred and how to fix it, and on top of this, more important and urgent work comes up. The defect now requires additional resources for the restoration of the context, and constant supply of some more important things to do makes it impossible to eliminate non-priority defects.

Another practical challenge is to estimate the size of the constantly growing defects queue. Ten defects — is it still tolerable? How about fifty? Five hundred? How can one compare errors of different priorities, significance or impact? Can a defect that was in the queue for a week, wait a bit longer? What if it was a month? Or a year? Taking into account that the defect queue is hidden somewhere deep in the ITSM tool, to become conscious of it already constitutes a problem. The problem becomes even more interesting when we add considerations like *There is no point to fix this error, since we plan to replace this component within six months anyway*. To make the picture even more realistic, we have to add that the error is likely to be in the queue for at least a year and *we plan to replace* does not mean *we will replace*. And not within six months, as a rule.

In DevOps, defects are fixed in a different way. In accordance with the principle *the system should always be in working order*, and to control the technical debt, most of the detected errors get priority to be fixed immediately — for example, within the same or the next sprint, if the team uses Scrum. In the case of minor defects, an extended time may be allocated, but it should not be too long and must be respected.

Like many other DevOps practices, immediate defect fixing requires a significant transformation of planning, prioritization and operations, and also serious changes in the core work principles. Many managers simply do not agree with the idea of immediate defect fixing. Likewise, previously they did not agree with the ITSM principle *All received calls should be logged*. In this case, one of the methods is to deal with the detected defects in the same way as with new functionality. Errors and user stories fall into a single queue and are treated equally. Indeed, the choice of a user story to implement is made on the same principles as the choice of an error to fix. Giving the new functionality a priority over error fixing is the same management decision made for the same IT system, same resources, same users. In this case, customers become involved in the management of technical debt, which greatly changes both the significance of this work and the responsibility for its results.

4.1.6 Processes are improved continuously

The way a conventional IT department changes its work processes is even worse. External consultants, or a working group of employees, or even a specialized unit develop a new guidance. As a rule, they describe a model that reflects the desired way of operations to some degree. Like any model, it will introduce a gap between the desired practice and its documented description. For example, it is difficult to envisage all possible situations and deviations, it is difficult to describe the motivational part, and it is difficult to ensure sufficient level of details without confusing everyone and turning employees into robots. The next gap between reality and documented guidance occurs when the actual performance turns out to be different from the expected. In some cases, employees will cut corners, in others they will try to work better than the instructions state. The third gap is created by the process automation, on which processes are highly dependent. In many cases, the process automation tool configuration is done significantly later than the new process is introduced. The work is already being done in the new way, but the automation system has not changed yet. Or, even worse, the work is not performed in the right way because it is not possible to change the automation system. I know a company where the average time for changes in the ITSM system goes up to two years, which causes delays in the process optimization.

All these gaps have an extremely negative impact on the work practice. Therefore, DevOps uses a different approach: all identified process deficiencies should be eliminated immediately. For example, if a script that runs the deployment pipeline does not work correctly, it must be fixed immediately. Moreover, in contrast to the traditional practice where problems can be postponed, DevOps recommends the problematic steps to be repeated as often as possible. This will allow to better understand how they should be improved, and to adjust the work accordingly.

4.1.7 Act as a startup

Some DevOps teams emerged in startups, with their specific culture, so unusual for corporate employees. Companies trying to implement DevOps, attempt to adopt the spirit of entrepreneurship and innovation. But what does this mean? What is the difference, can it be articulated? It turns out that it can: the key differences are in the following table:

Feature	Traditional corporate culture	Culture of startups
Management style	Command, authoritarian	Autonomous
Attitude to change	Conservatism	Experiments
Organizational structure	Functional hierarchy	Network
Focus on outputs	Project-oriented	Product-oriented
Change model	Waterfall	Agile, iterative
System architecture	Monolithic, carefully designed	Loosely coupled, microservice
Technology preferences	Patented, proprietary	Open source

Fig. 4.1 Difference in the culture of traditional corporations and startups

It seems that for all of the above features, a DevOps culture is very different from the regular one, which, of course, is an obstacle for direct and rapid change in the style of work in traditional organizations. The above table summarizes the main differences, which allows us to move on to a detailed review of the individual DevOps practices. Remember that many of them are, so to say, borrowed from other sources, which does not diminish the importance of each of these sources, and neither of DevOps.

4.2 Unusual teams

In the table above, the *Culture of startups* column shows some differences that make the use of traditional functional management impossible or extremely difficult. In particular, the autonomy, product orientation and network organizational structure are pushing for a revision of the approach to grouping specialists for optimal effectiveness. Teams, not structural units come to the forefront.

A DevOps team is an amazing combat unit. It is responsible for a small but clearly defined part of an IT system or IT infrastructure. Having this focus, team members gradually and inevitably become experts in the subject area, while remaining fully responsible for it.

A DevOps team is not a temporary project team; on the contrary, it is formed for the long term. Moreover, usually the lifetime of the team is not determined in advance and is not fixed. The team works in its area of responsibility as long as the area remains relevant. If the trajectory is changed, the team 'turns' along with the area of responsibility; and if this area is abandoned, the team switches to another. There is no established view among practitioners as to whether it is necessary to break up teams from time to time. On the one hand, the distribution of the team members of one successful team between the others allows for faster exchange of competences and experience. However, many experts object that the time and resources spent on forming an effective and established team could be reinvested in other tasks, while retaining the team; they suggest that knowledge sharing can and should be done regardless of the formation of teams, and in other ways.

Team members work in the team for 100% of their working time: no more sharing of resources, combining duties here and there, covering for a sick employee of another department and the like. Full commitment of each team member simplifies work coordination, removes dependencies on external factors and excludes the opportunity to find excuses in another workload. On the other hand, this approach increases HR costs (see Section 1.3.1 *Decrease time to market*).

DevOps teams are cross-functional; this means that a team should be able to fully perform all the work in the value stream of its area of responsibility. This is the only way to make possible a common and accurate understanding of the Definition of Done; only this way can ensure that all tasks are completed, and the unfinished work is entirely eliminated.

The team size is important. On one hand, it cannot be too small: a small team cannot become cross-functional, as described above. On the other hand, teams of twenty or more people are difficult to coordinate and will either require forming of management levels, or they will tend to fall apart into subteams. In addition, large teams incur additional costs for communication and the inevitable loss of information between members. All this affects the speed of work.

The small size and the need for cross-functionality put forward an additional requirement for DevOps teams: team members should be as versatile as possible. A clear specialization is familiar: this is a programmer, that is a tester, and that is an information security specialist. But a DevOps team requires the boundaries to be erased: ideally, everyone should be able to do the work of everyone. This does not mean that everyone will become equally bad developers or database administrators, for example. It is clear that the expertise of employees in certain areas can and should be deep. However, universality allows team members to help each other, exchange competences, and understand at the expert level how everything is organized. All this balances the workload and creates a joint responsibility of the team as a unit, rather than individual gurus and heroes.

There is no formal leader, no coordinator or supervisor among a small number of DevOps team members. The team should be able to independently solve all emerging management issues and to seek support from experts or mentors in difficult cases. By analogy with Scrum, the product owner does not have a larger voice than any other member of the team, and the Scrum Master is not a dedicated person: it's just a role transferred from one team member to another from time to time. In other words, this should be a self-organizing team, which is quite achievable for teams of small size.

It is important that all team members are physically collocated. A constant face-to-face contact is necessary; remote e-communications are not enough. There are serious reasons for this requirement: first, the 'write-read' communications hide the emotional component, regardless of the media (e-mail, instant message, formal document), the accuracy of the wording, and the presence of emoticons. In quite obvious cases the recipient is clear as to whether they were praised or held against, but in all other situations, the main emotional message of the sender remains behind the scenes. There are cases when seemingly innocent written comments caused a storm of indignation, and comparison to certain famous characters was perceived as a public insult. Good, if such reaction is immediately noted! However, it is worth remembering that many of the IT-professionals are introverts, who tend to hold grudges. And if one adds almost limitless technical capabilities combined with access to the source code and the production environment, to the made up negative emotions, the resulting mixture can be highly explosive.

Second, the location of the entire team in the same room makes daily contact with everyone inevitable. An e-mail in the inbox can be ignored for weeks. Phone calls may simply not be accepted, referring to high workload, meetings and so on. And the inconvenient questions of a colleague standing right there have to be answered immediately: the programmer now cannot hide from the tester, and the tester from the operation specialist. Poor quality work, defects, incidents will not only be identified and registered in some information system, they will also be promptly corrected, with the joint efforts of the team. This style of groupwork does not require a leader, coordinator or other navigator.

A DevOps team is responsible for the tools it uses. How to build a pipeline, which technologies or versions of libraries to use — all these questions are in the team's area of responsibility. The team should be able to assess the consequences of any changes that are being made. These statements do not revoke the need to follow corporate standards, including those in the areas of architecture, information security and audit.

> As an example of a corporate standard that is understandable for all teams, let's recall the famous Jeff Bezos's decision to change from a monolithic to microservice architecture in 2001[35]. His message sent to the technical specialists said:
> 1. All teams will henceforth expose their data and functionality through service interfaces.
> 2. Teams must communicate with each other through these interfaces.
> 3. There will be no other form of interprocess communication allowed.
> 4. It doesn't matter what technology they use.
> 5. All service interfaces, without exception, must be designed from the ground up to be externalizable. That is to say, the team must plan and design to be able to expose the interface to developers in the outside world. No exceptions.
> 6. Anyone who doesn't do this will be fired.

The described features of DevOps teams lead to the difficulty of scaling: there is a need for coordination of work in different areas, which is especially important when using a common IT infrastructure. The presence of several dozen teams provokes the introduction of a management layer, which to a certain extent goes against attempts to increase speed and reduce waste. These difficulties may seem to be overwhelming, while they do not exist in the usual functional structure. Indeed, it seems very easy to scale the traditional organizational structure: you can add a department, you can appoint a manager there; you can play politics and swap managers; with the company growth, you can increase the number of management levels accordingly; you can introduce the institution of deputies and the combination of positions, and so on. However, it is clear that such tricks have a whole set of shortcomings, hiding and masking real problems of interaction, slowing down work and increasing waste.

So, let's sum up the key features of the DevOps teams:

---

[35] https://plus.google.com/+RipRowan/posts/eVeouesvaVX

Key Practices

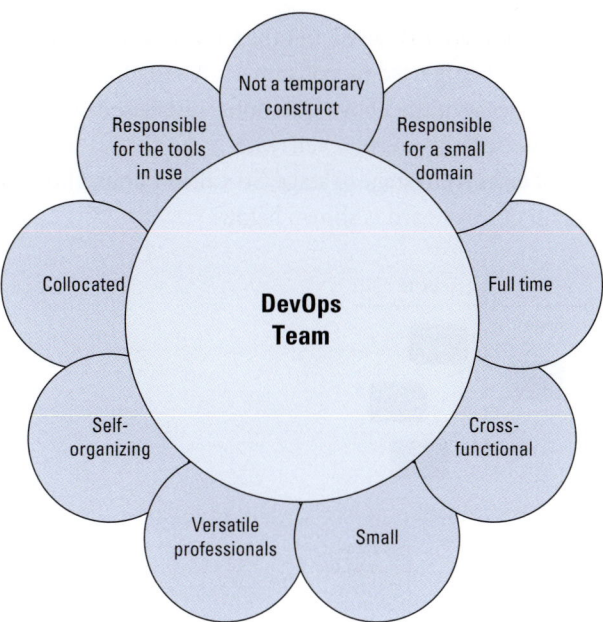

Fig. 4.2   Key features of the DevOps teams

4.3   Work visualization

As already mentioned in Section 2.1.2 *Challenges* of Section 2.1 *Lean production*, the work in IT, unlike production, is mostly intangible. You cannot touch the products, you do not assess the degree of its readiness by looking at the *partially ready product or item,* and in turn, it is hard to understand whether there is an overflow from the size of the queue. This intangibility prevents staff and managers from knowing at any given time the answers to such key questions as:
- How many tasks are currently accepted (so we are working on them) and what are these (which items exactly are we working on right now)?
- Which step is accumulating the work, forming a bottleneck that does not allow the rest of the chain to work effectively?
- Which areas have potentially insufficient capacity and will soon slow down the others?
- At what points or stages of our value stream are the resources nearly exhausted or close to full capacity?
- What tasks are stuck, so that they do not have chances to be completed in this iteration?
- What remains to be done for the task that has not been completed?
- If we do not have time to do all the work that was accepted in this iteration, what part of it is worth trying to complete to get the maximum possible useful result?

In fact, we are talking about ensuring the flow of the stream (see Section 3.1 *Value stream*), for which the principles and methods of the Theory of Constraints are fully applicable. At the same time, not only the development part is considered, but the whole chain, the entire pipeline, end-to-end, down to the software being used by consumers. A visualization tool can support the flow and help to find answers to the above questions. List-based systems, though quite popular, do not fully cope with the task, even with a dashboard add-on installed. They hardly display the flow of tasks from stage to stage. So-called Kanban boards are more appealing; the simplest version of this board is shown below:

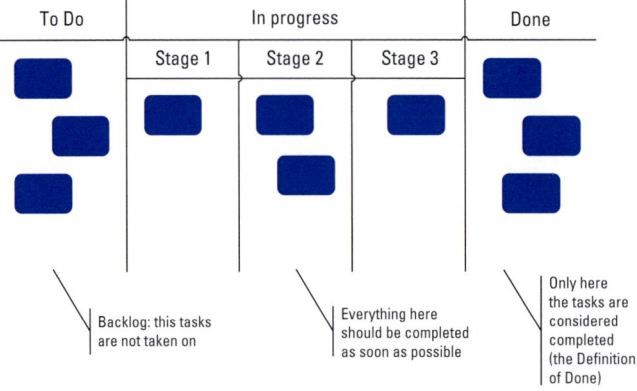

Fig. 4.3   Example of a Kanban board

The backlog for the whole team is entered on the left, in the *To do* column. Then, from left to right, there are work stages where tasks gradually move; this area is often referred to as *In progress*. The final point of the process, the *Done* column is on the right. A few important remarks from advanced DevOps teams practice can be added to this relatively primitive notation.

First, putting the task in the backlog does not mean taking on the work, as opposed to the generally accepted practice. The task in the backlog means literally the following: this is a good idea, it *can* be implemented when and if the decision is made. However, as soon as the person responsible for the first stage takes a task from the backlog, they immediately accept responsibility for its speedy execution, on behalf of the whole team.

Second, the tasks are prioritized only once, when transferred from the backlog to the first stage. At this point, potential benefits, required resources, urgency, and many other parameters can and should be evaluated. It is worth noting that there are many methods to determine priorities, and not all of them imply a detailed analysis of the listed parameters. One of the most interesting ways to manage the queue will be discussed in Section 4.10 *Task prioritization*.

So, as soon as the decision to accept the task is made, it is not possible to ignore it at the next stages: everything that started its movement along the pipeline, must carry on to the end. The cancellation of one task in favour of adding another one is unacceptable, because work in progress is one of the types of waste that should be opposed. As a consequence of this practice, all participants of the chain, except the first one, do not need to spend time prioritizing the incoming tasks, because the priorities have already been defined and should not be changed.

Third, a watchful reader has probably noticed that the output of the previous stage is the input of the next. Thus, a queue is formed before each stage, which makes it possible to visually assess the number of tasks in every section.

And finally, the use of Kanban boards allows to build a so-called pull system. Usually, the one who completed the previous stage, pushes the work to the next one in the chain, trying to somehow influence the acceptance, the speed of processing and other parameters of his neighbour on the right — in fact, loading them with the responsibility. On the contrary, with the pulling system after completing the current task, the responsible member of the team takes on the next one from the queue and embarks on the work. This allows for a smoother flow, more efficient use of resources, and eliminates the need for coordination, thus greatly reducing the role of supervisors and other operational managers.

We should note one more unexpected application of the Kanban boards: they can be used as an indicator of incorrect use of the DevOps approach. For example, if the prioritization is wrong, the entry into the chain quickly becomes overloaded, leading to confusion in all other sections. In this case, it is clear that the flow is not what should be optimized. The principles of prioritization and management of the queue need to be understood, as well as the fundamental approach to task management: pull system vs push system (the latter, of course, contradicts the very idea of using Kanban and Lean principles). Another example is attempts to apply Kanban boards for support and operations units, without changing the principles of their operation. In this case the mess is also guaranteed due to the large number of tasks to display and track, that makes the board unreadable. It is often combined with a fairly formal approach to moving tasks across the board: the task status in the system is changed, so the task is moved to the next column, but the next operator did not actually accept it. All this has still very little to do with the flow and its management.

Let's summarize the benefits of visualization:
- allows to build a pull system, which in turn:
  - improves the workflow;
  - reduces downtime;
  - reduces the need for coordination;
- improves the visibility of the tasks in progress;
- improves understanding of the remaining amount of work and the current status;
- improves prioritization;
- reduces the number of hand-offs;
- helps to identify inefficiencies.

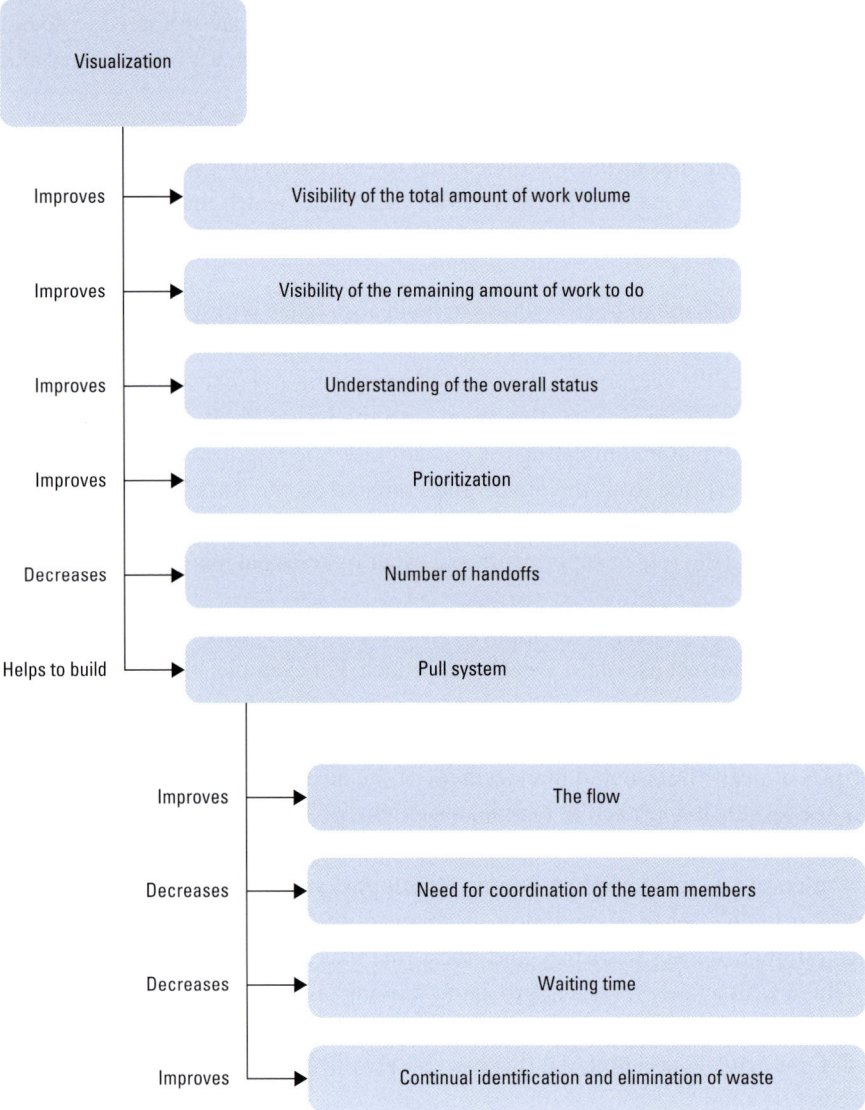

Fig. 4.4 The effect of visualization

4.4 Limit the WIP

Traditional practice implies that tasks come from various sources asynchronously. As a rule, a specialist is involved in several processes, allocating part of his working time for each of them. In addition to predictable processes, ad-hoc tasks come from the manager, from dissatisfied business units, from colleagues who need, as usual, "just ten minutes." In many companies, automation tools enable creation of a wonderful list of all the tasks assigned to a particular specialist:

My tasks

Task	Comments	Priority	Deadline
User call	Xxxxxxxxxxxxxxxxxxxxxxxxx	Normal	Yesterday
Incident	Xxxxxxxxxxxxxxxxxxxxxxxxx	High	Yesterday
Change request	Xxxxxxxxxxxxxxxxxxxxxxxxx	Scheduled	Yesterday
Work order	Xxxxxxxxxxxxxxxxxxxxxxxxx	Low	Yesterday
Incident	Xxxxxxxxxxxxxxxxxxxxxxxxx	Critical	Today
User call	Xxxxxxxxxxxxxxxxxxxxxxxxx	Normal	Today
Work order	Xxxxxxxxxxxxxxxxxxxxxxxxx	High	Tomorrow
Work order	Xxxxxxxxxxxxxxxxxxxxxxxxx	Normal	Tomorrow

Fig. 4.5 Example of a task list for one operator

The list is wonderful in many ways:
- it is never complete, some of the tasks and assignments are recorded on post-its, in a notebook, in the short-term memory, or simply nowhere;
- some of the tasks are planned, and the others are ad-hoc;
- all the work on this list will never be done on time for a million of different reasons, despite the agreed priorities and deadlines;
- many tasks will be on the list for quite a long time (months, or even years), causing the list's relevance to decrease.

The long list of tasks leads to chaos. This chaos is related to the frequent review of priorities by the specialist *("what should I do now?")*, frequent switching between tasks *("I do not have time to do this, I'll do that instead")*, frequent changes in priorities due to external factors *("a more urgent task emerged, I will leave this one for now"* and similar issues. In some companies, the common practice of prioritization is reduced to HiPPO: Highest Paid Person's Opinion.

The cause of these problems is multitasking. There is an opinion that an ordinary person is able to do several intellectual tasks at the same time, however, studies of recent decades, as well as practice, show that this is not the case. In most cases, IT employees do only one job at a time; if one tries performing several tasks simultaneously, then one spends most of one's time switching between them. Switching takes time, to which one needs to add at least time for re-prioritization and time for changing the context. Measurements show a multiple increase in the duration of tasks in a multi-tasking mode compared to single-tasking.

The working method to oppose to this practice is to limit the number of tasks in progress. On one hand, it sounds strange: does it mean that the specialist will not accept a new task, which is part of his/her job responsibilities? On the other hand, it is an effective mechanism for ensuring an even flow of tasks and delivering results within a predictable timeframe. The essence of this practice is that on each stage of the value stream artificial restrictions are established regarding the number of tasks performed simultaneously or on the total number of tasks accepted (WIP Limit, Work in Progress/Process Limit). In the extreme case, down to one task per each workplace in any given time. The total number of tasks in the entire stream is limited in the same way.

This practice perfectly supports the principle of pulling, which has already been discussed above. Indeed, with the WIP restriction, the person responsible for the previous stage of work, has no way to transfer the task to the next stage: they just inform their colleague down the stream that they have completed their part. The next one in the chain completes their current task, and then proceeds to the next one — exactly at the moment when they become available for a new job.

This practice may lead to situations where there is no work on the individual stages of the stream: they are waiting for the completion of the previous stages. In a usual IT department the decision would be made to do something else, load the staff with some new work — just because employees should not be idle! They get salaries, and therefore should work one hundred, and preferably one hundred and twenty percent. At the end of the day, the maximum utilization of resources, human resources included, is one of the most important objectives of every manager. But not in DevOps, though.

The rule *It is better to do at least something than not to do anything* does not work here, even more so, it is considered extremely harmful. Doing work that does not have a customer, is a waste. Upgrading servers to new versions only because new versions are available, is a waste. To take up a task during the idle time just to leave it unfinished later, is a waste. Instead, it is better to take the downtime at one stage as an indicator of an overload at the other, and immediately take response measures. These measures can be both operational (assistance to the overloaded colleague) and more systemic (elimination of a bottleneck in the stream). The main focus is to ensure the flow, and in this case the analogy with the flow of the river works well: when everything is good and steady, the speed of the flow is also steady. At the time of high water too much of it gathers at the entry, it cannot flow through the channel; the river will burst its banks with inevitable loss of water and damage to the territories along its banks. On the other hand, if in a usual situation the river gets shallow, then somewhere upstream there is an obstacle; it must be found and removed in order to restore the normal, steady and predictable flow.

Some experts, such as Jez Humble, recommend that restrictions are set so that they intentionally create inconvenience. At the time when someone in the chain does not have work to do, and resources are free, a passionate desire emerges to relax the restrictions at the previous stages of the flow, so that at least some work could be sent downstream. To prevent this desire and focus on bottlenecks elimination, experts recommend setting constraints that bring some pain, but make the system explicitly limited.

Returning to the resource utilization, it is worth noting that WIP restrictions that are set correctly and regularly adjusted are a good tool to balance intensity and productivity of work. The fact is that there is a correlation between the WIP and the average lead time:

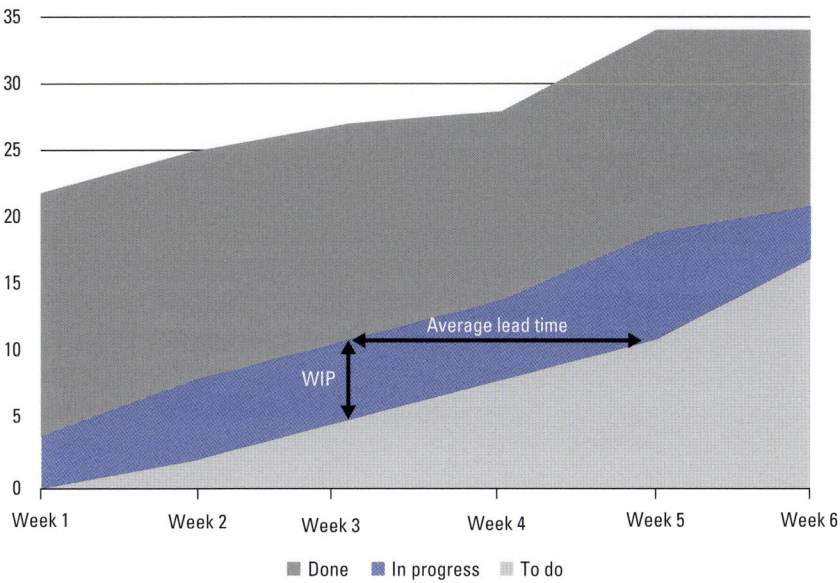

Fig. 4.6 Cumulative flow diagram

Another important aspect is predictability of the output. In many cases, despite all efforts to assess the complexity of tasks, it can be very difficult to estimate how much time this work will take in the end, that is, to forecast the release time. Two tools come in handy: accumulated statistics on the speed of the team and management of WIP. By tightening the constraint, it is possible to achieve shorter lead times to the detriment of staff utilization, and vice versa. Therefore, the managers' work is dramatically changing with DevOps.

The consequences of limiting the WIP are summed up in Figure 4.7.

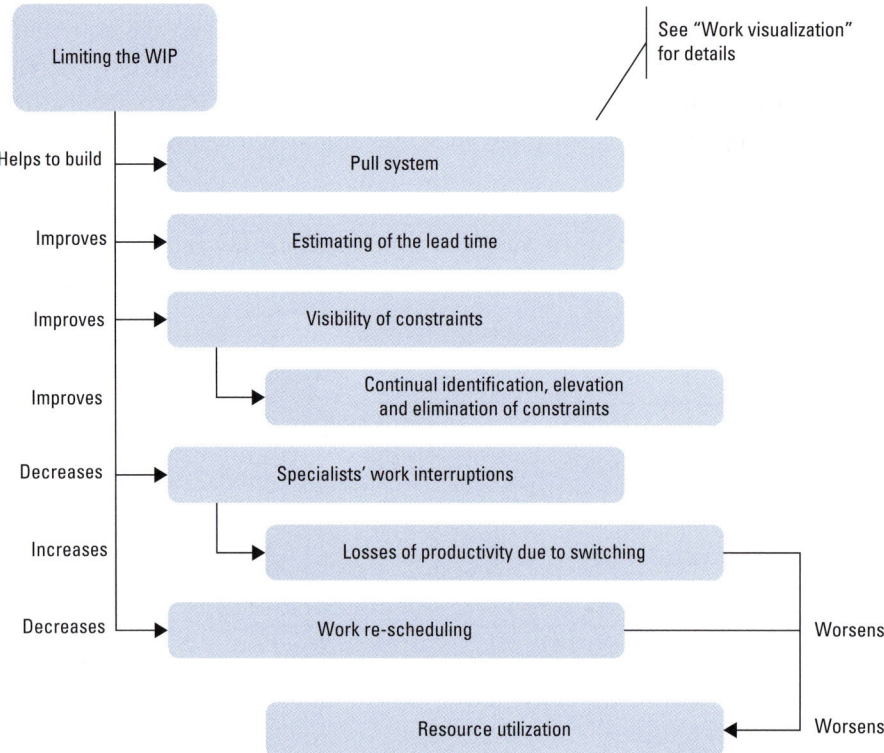

Fig. 4.7 The effect of limiting the WIP

4.5 Reduce batch size

Suppose there is a need to make and subsequently test several identical products. Here is one way to organize the work: we make the first product, we pass it for testing, at this time we start making the second product, which we then pass for testing, and so on. The second option: we make all the products at once, and then pass them for testing. It is common to find an erroneous judgment that the second method is always more effective than the first. However, practice shows that the effectiveness depends on the total batch size, product variability, the required speed of having the products done, the time for equipment adjustment and other factors, and hence there is no common definite answer.

However, in the area of information technology, the option with smaller batches shows better results, for the following reasons. First, large batches are rarely the same in size, in contrast to the small ones — even down to a so-called Single-piece Flow. Small batches of the same size improve the rhythm of work; it becomes more steady and predictable in all areas. Second, the time of the first delivery and the total lead time are minimized by decreasing the waiting time in the value stream. Third, small batches reduce the total volume of tasks in progress. Fourth, the number of defects is reduced: the entire batch will have to be redone if there is an error. The smaller the batch, the smaller the waste from rework. All this positively influences the key aspects of DevOps: the lead time, the workload and the quality of the products.

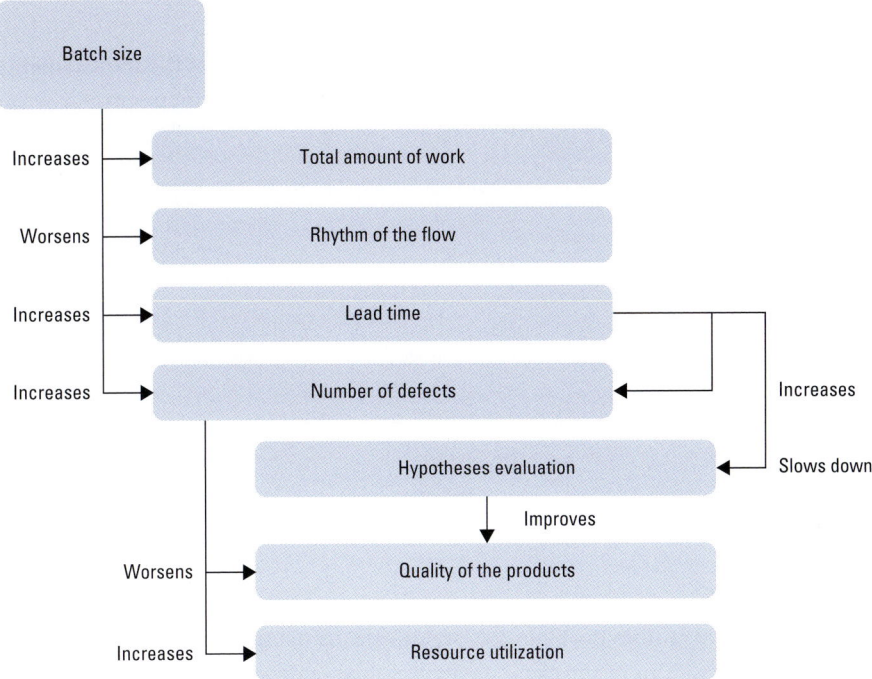

Fig. 4.8 The effect of decreasing the batch size

In the usual work of an IT department, batches can be difficult to detect. One of the striking examples is that programmers execute large tasks for several days, whereas the results are saved in the version control system only once and at the very end. The recommended alternative is to save independent intermediate results throughout the entire duration of the work, at least once a day. In a well-configured pipeline, each saving will trigger the following steps, for example, testing, which will provide early feedback and prevent defects. Due to the small volume of each change, it will be easier to correct the identified errors.

4.6 Mind the operational requirements

In IT departments where development and operation divisions are separate, the questions of providing the functionality required by the customer tend to find their answers. Developers are interested in the customer describing what they want to get, and are ready to fulfil these requirements. In turn, the operation department is interested in a normal, working relationship with the users, which can be achieved only if the users can do their job using the functionality provided.

Traditionally the problematic area is the so-called non-functional requirements (NFR): availability, reliability, scalability, maintainability, security and the like. These primarily affect an IT operations department, where incidents are tackled, their root causes are investigated, the growing user base and dissatisfied consumers are dealt with... And all of this occurs amid strict resource constraints, which relax slower than the requirements for IT operations grow. That said, the development department can focus primarily on functional requirements, ignoring the NFR to some extent.

Fig. 4.9 A usual set of -ities associated with non-functional requirements

The traditional solution to this problem for organizations using the waterfall model, is to try involving IT operations at the early stages of software development. The word 'try' is not applied accidentally, since only a few companies have made significant progress in this involvement. The solution applied by the adepts of agile development is prioritization of non-functional requirements along with the functional ones, namely: following the same procedure, with the same degree of importance, with the same level of control. This practice is certainly better than the traditional one.

DevOps goes a little further. First, the role of the product owner expands. In Scrum, it is a person who is the most interested in the product, or its representative, but with a certain bias or limitation, to the product features. DevOps experts suggest to consider the product owner as interested in a fully operational IT system, including both functional and other requirements. This radically changes NFR's significance and shifts the focus of the team towards a working product, where *working* is not limited to the agreed functionality.

Second, some DevOps visionaries insist on abandoning the customary name of non-functional requirements that has a negative connotation of secondary or lesser importance, and replace it with operational requirements (OR)[36].

---

[36] To illustrate the importance of operational requirements, a special phrase was invented: "...*OR this doesn't deploy into production*".

Third, it is proposed to completely revise the approach to IT systems' availability and performance. In the legacy systems, the focus was on designing and building for high reliability: systems should fail as rarely as possible. The expensive specialized software and hardware solutions were used to meet the requirements, such as: redundancy, backups, hot swapping and the like. These solutions were usually provided by well-known vendors, they used proprietary technologies, with long-term and expensive support and maintenance contracts attached. In DevOps, the main focus is shifted from reliability to resilience, or anti-fragility: the system should be able to detect and correct failures and to restore normal operations without significant loss of performance and without affecting the users. The system itself is built on the basis of a large number of relatively cheap and easy to replace components, using distributed data storage, parallel computing and similar technologies, preferably opensource. The practice of deliberate and continual introduction of chaos and destruction into the production environment was mentioned in Section 1.3.3 *Eliminate fragility*.

So, it becomes obvious that the work with operational requirements is organized in a quite different way in DevOps. Moreover, there is an interesting and fashionable practice of demonstrating the time of continuous operation and the systems status in a form understandable to end users, as shown below:

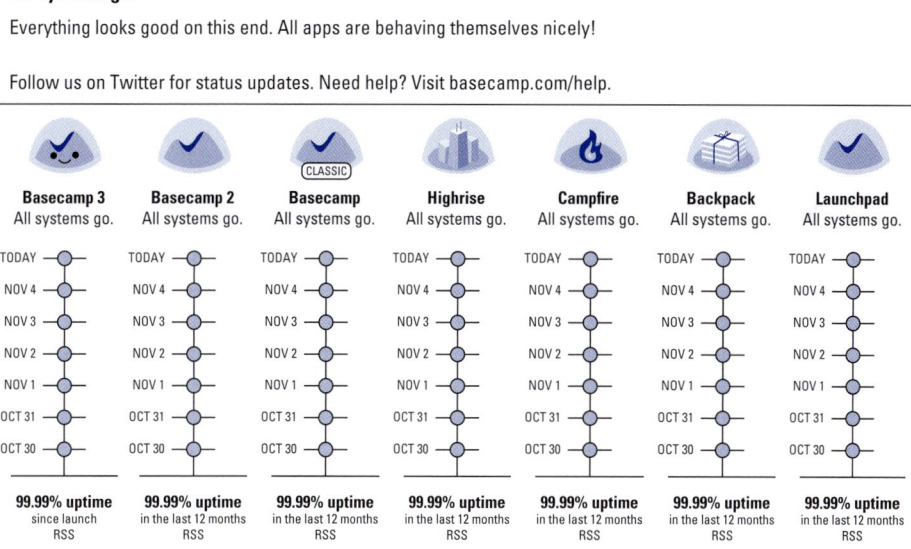

Fig. 4.10 An example of a public web page that displays the current systems status at Basecamp[37]

Pages of this type enhance trust between DevOps teams and users and demonstrate the achievements throughout the service lifecycle, rather than during the development phase, only. In addition, a single source of system status information allows to prevent

---

37 https://status.basecamp.com/

massive calls, emails and other user messages in case of a system failure. And finally, the uptime information here is a direct analogy to the well-known *146 days without an accident* boards in production environments; it improves the morale of employees, gives them a sense of security and collective responsibility.

4.7 Early detection and correction of defects

The greatest losses associated with information technology occur when defects affect the production environment: users cannot do their work, because the system is unavailable, or it works intermittently, or some of the functionality is broken. As we already discussed in Section 3.2 *Deployment pipeline*, DevOps pays a lot of attention to preventing defects from coming into the production environment. Moreover, a closer analysis reveals that, in addition to business losses, the cost of identifying and eliminating defects grows as it moves from start to the end of the pipeline. See Figure 4.11.

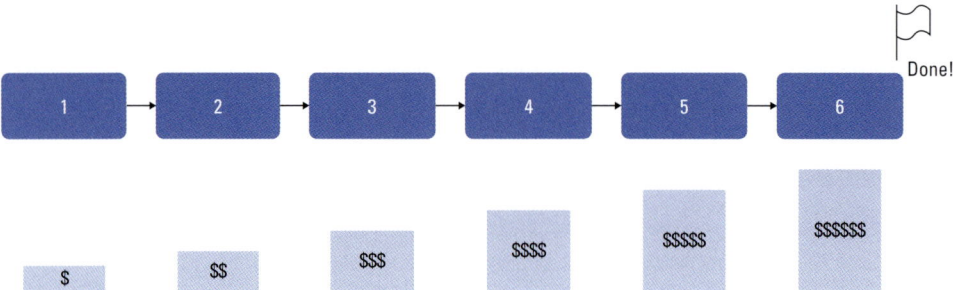

Fig. 4.11 Losses and costs increase with late detection of defects

Indeed, to detect a defect in the fourth stage, we should have already spent resources on the left, in stages 1, 2 and 3 — for example, to create the required test environments and to run the tests. These resources cannot be returned, as well as the time; this, of course, will negatively affect the lead time. The problem becomes particularly serious when not all parts of the pipeline are fully automated; for example, if one of the stages requires manual testing, then the cost of such testing increases significantly. It turns out that the sooner defects are detected, the better — both in terms of costs and performance of the pipeline. There is a need for early feedback, which allows returning to the previous stages as close as possible to the beginning of the pipeline. One of the practices for this is called *Shift left*: testing is organized in a way that maximizes the detection of the most common errors in the early steps. This requires increased testing on the first stages of the pipeline, which slows down these stages, so a certain balance should be observed.

Note that the greatest gain is achieved when testing is automated as much as possible. It can be said that in the absolute DevOps pipeline, the role and work of the testers is changing: their main task is not to perform the tests, but to develop. This change confirms the old and still relevant principle: intellectual work belongs to humans, while repetitive routine operations can be delegated to machines.

In addition, the practice where the test environments correspond to the production environment as accurately as possible, supports fast detection of defects. Situations where testing during the pipeline was flawless, but in production environment the application does not work properly, are dangerous and lead to losses. This means that we should do our best to ensure that the test environments not only fully reflect the production environment, but also are created in the same way. As it was shown in *Automated configuration management*, this is possible nowadays.

4.8 Managed, not controlled improvements and innovations

Discussing the need for DevOps in Section 1.3.2 *Reduce technical debt*, we touched an important issue of continual accumulation of non-optimal solutions. In the natural course of affairs, technical debt tends to increase, unless special measures and actions are taken. This is also true for methods of work and management: processes, procedures, agreements, and so on. Left to themselves, processes begin to deteriorate, employees cut corners not only in technical solutions, but also in the way they work. Moreover, the dynamics of modern life suggests that external factors change quite often and what worked fine yesterday — whether it is a software solution or a procedure — is less effective today.

Finally, information technology itself is flying forward in leaps and bounds. Since 2010, ThoughtWorks, a company that is quite prominent in the market of effective software development, has been publishing a special report about this every six months: the so-called Technology Radar[38]. It lists more than a hundred items, grouped into four areas: Techniques, Platforms, Tools and Languages & Frameworks. For example, among the techniques in 2017 there were API as a product, serverless architecture, virtual reality beyond gaming; among the platforms — Apache Mesos, AWS Lambda, PlatformIO; among the tools — Airflow, HashCorp Vault, Terraform and finally, among the languages and frameworks — Python 3, Elixir, Angular 2 and others.

Each of the items belongs to one of four classes: to adopt bravely, to try, to assess for the future, or to put on hold and wait. On many points an explanation is given. Therefore, a qualified team of subject matter experts carries out quite labour-intensive work on the analysis of new technologies completely free of charge for consumers. Comparing several recent reports, one can see how new technologies develop dynamically (or die). Technology opportunities emerge constantly, and many of them can potentially bring a serious return.

---

38 https://www.thoughtworks.com/radar

So, technical debt needs to be reduced, work needs to be improved, and new technologies mastered. The modern IT department cannot afford to engage in these important tasks in the background during some time free from the core work: with this approach, it will turn out at best to remain in place and at worst (and more likely) to degrade. That is why DevOps implies a continual improvement and innovation. In different companies, this practice can be completely different. Here are just a few examples.

Some companies start with the allocation of a certain proportion of working time for the improvement; the expression *20% tax* can be found more and more often in publications. It is clear that the number is pulled out of a hat and it can hardly be the same for all organizations, but there are some justified estimates, too. For example, the SAFe model invites teams to work in so-called program increments of 8 to 12 weeks. The final stage of each increment is an iteration dedicated to innovation and planning. For the sake of fairness, it should be noted that the same iteration includes completion of unfinished work from previous sprints, final integration and testing, and planning of the next increment; thus, only a few days remain from the initial two weeks, and the allocated time for innovation will make from 1.5% to 15% of the total increment duration. Let's consider this estimate as the lowest reasonable. The highest reasonable can be taken from the words of Marty Cagan, who in the late 1990s experienced a technical debt crisis at eBay, and then presented his thoughts in his book *Inspired: How to Create Products Customers Love*[39]. According to Cagan, in some difficult cases it will be necessary to give for improvement up to 30% or more, but teams that allocate less than 20%, cause mistrust. It is interesting, that many experts recommend banning any normal work during the time allocated for improvement: neither programming, nor testing, nor deployment are allowed.

Another practice is so-called Kaizen Blitz. In this case, the time for improvement may not be planned in advance, but is allocated as necessary. It is also suggested to involve external participants: they may be other team's members, or guest experts. It is believed that an external view can help to move the problem from a dead end and to find solutions that are not visible from within the team. The actual blitzes take from one to several days and are focused on eliminating the identified shortcomings and bottlenecks. Therefore, each blitz is expected to have a very definite and tangible result: in the worst case, this is a list of actions to be taken, and in the best the fixed errors.

Some companies combine time allocation and use of external resources, also putting high hopes on the knowledge and experience sharing within the company. For example, at Target, teams move to a specially designated area (office) for a full calendar month. Dedicated mentors join them to help reorganize work on existing tasks to achieve more with the same resources in less time. The company has allocated resources for simultaneous acceleration of up to eight teams. It is assumed that in this month the team will not only

---

39 Cagan, M., *Inspired: How To Create Products Customers Love*, 2008, ISBN 978-0981690407

complete the assigned work, but will also learn new ways, methods and techniques, and will be able to transfer their new knowledge to other employees upon return.

Finally, the so-called 'hackathons' are becoming more widespread. A hackathon is a timeframe specially allocated for exploring new technologies and attempting to create new products and tools. It is understood and accepted that not everything created will have a completed shape, or have commercial potential. However, there are more and more examples where prototypes of new user applications were developed at hackathons, and later became successful products. There are cases where technologies used internally were significantly revised to simplify the increasingly complicated architecture, remove rigid links, and get rid of accumulated dependencies, and so on.

To conclude this section on the continual improvement and innovation, it is necessary to make two important observations:
- this practice should be managed, rather than left unattended;
- this practice in your company is likely to be different from other organizations.

4.9 Funding that enables innovations

The availability of timely and sufficient funding is a prerequisite for any activity. Traditionally, decisions to allocate funds are made on the basis of medium- and long-term planning aligned to budget cycles. This approach worked well ten years ago, but today it creates obstacles for companies striving to become leaders in innovation. What is wrong with it?

To begin with, usually funding is built as a cycle — repetitive (as a rule, annual) iterations set a rhythm for budget planning and accounting. The very presence of rhythm is a positive factor, the trouble is that this rhythm is different from what a modern company needs. Indeed, is it possible to predict with certainty what impact in twelve months' time will have ideas that have not even been put into development? Is it possible to confidently calculate the costs for such a long period? As described in Section 1.3.1 *Decrease time to market*, in many cases, confidence in the chosen direction can emerge only in the course of the movement, and turns on the way are inevitable. It's quite sad if the company's budget cycle is tied to the time of tax reporting. Perhaps, it is very convenient for the departments responsible for book-keeping and tax accounting, but it should be remembered that these units do not create much value for the organization; they are secondary to the goals, mission, customers, products and partners of the company. It turns out that the need to comply with certain external requirements determines the way of the business planning. Readers familiar with the basics of management accounting, will agree that this distortion should be eliminated; however, it is a practice adopted by the vast majority of modern enterprises.

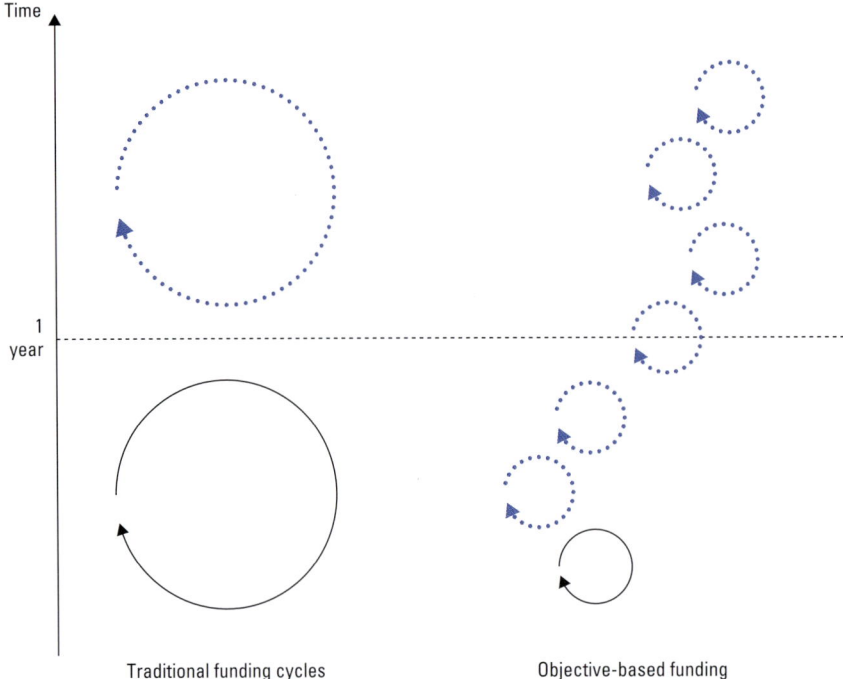

Fig. 4.12 The funding cycles do not coincide in time and in the direction, and rarely can be synchronized with each other

The second fundamental difficulty arises from the widespread use of project-based funding: it is believed that in projects the costs can be carefully planned and then controlled, and the return can be predicted. However, for a large number of modern initiatives, traditional project management makes little sense:
- the product that the organization seeks to deliver cannot be accurately specified in advance and will change many times over the course of the work;
- after the formal completion of the project, the product will only begin its life cycle, which consists of constant improvement and corrections based on new experience gained in using and responding to customers;
- DevOps experts do not recommend dismissing established DevOps teams, nor do they recommend involving part-time employees.

Therefore, the practice of funding products rather than projects would be more appropriate, and this means a completely different way of budgeting and resource planning.

Having mentioned the subject of resources, we cannot ignore another typical problem: traditional budgeting approaches imply tough competition between departments or teams. It is clear that resources are limited, but DevOps regards the principles of cooperation, joint work of departments and teams, free knowledge sharing and expertise as of paramount importance. If at the level of funding rules (that is, resource allocation) an organization introduces the need to fight and compete with colleagues, then one should not be surprised to find a corporate culture, where isolation of individual groups is the norm.

In the old days, when the complexity of the systems and the speed of change were lower, traditional methods of funding worked relatively well (except for cases when budgeting was used as a tool of restriction, not prioritization). Nowadays, the barriers created by this hinder innovation. An alternative approach that allows to get a high return on investment is the establishment of stable product (or service) teams and funding them on an ongoing basis with a certain degree of freedom in choosing their strategy, implementation methods and priorities in the area of responsibility.

Of course, what has been said above does not mean that there are no restrictions, for example, on expenses. On the contrary, the experience of some startups shows that in the situation of strict accounting and expense control, miracles of ingenuity can occur as well as new, unique technical solutions that other teams with different principles of resource planning could not come up with. Life proves again and again that unlimited funds and an endless calendar are still not enough to create competitive products, for which consumers will be queueing up.

The alternative approach, which DevOps borrows to a certain extent from modern lean enterprise management practices implies a high-level definition of long-term goals, more precise planning of immediate actions and constant adjustment of short-term plans to ensure the right direction.

In a simpler case, already mentioned above, the funding principles would change from project-based funding to allocating funds for each team. The process described by Jez Humble[40] is more complicated, but also much more productive:
- *Orient* stage: search and evaluation of the idea without spending time and resources on the development of an accurate and complex business model;
- *Explore* stage: allocation of a fixed time and budget; team building, development of a minimum viable product, or MVP ;
- in case the product proved attractive at the previous stage, the next stage is *Exploit*: preservation of the team, expansion of funding, product development, search for additional opportunities.

The main purpose of this process is to select interesting ideas; to invest limited resources in some of them with the expectation that most ideas will not take off, but some will certainly show a significant result. Note that many technology business incubators where innovations are treated as a pipeline, follow the same principles.

---

[40] Humble, J., J. Molesky and B. O'Reilly, *Lean Enterprise: How High Performance Organizations Innovate at Scale*, 2015, ISBN 978-1449368425

> The above-mentioned concept of MVP is often used completely incorrectly. Many believe that MVP is something done quick and dirty, some minimal functionality, working somehow without obvious and noticeable defects, to demonstrate the prototype to investors. A sort of early alpha version of the product.
>
> However, Eric Ries,[41] the author of the term MVP, described it as a *strategy of investing the minimum possible resources to obtain through testing and training the maximum possible new information for making a decision based on objective data: to continue in the same direction, to change the course or to discard the idea.*
>
> Marty Cagan adds significant MVP characteristics:
> 1. *customers should want to buy or use the product;*
> 2. *customers should be able to understand how to use the product;*
> 3. *we must be able to produce the complete product when and if such decision is made.*
>
> Many focus only on the last statement, hence on functionality. In fact, all three are important.

4.10 Task prioritization

An area that often causes difficulties is the prioritization of tasks in the queue at the entry to the value stream. A traditional approach calls to analyse tasks, evaluate them, compare and prioritize, obtain approval or permission; all this before before undertaking the work. All these actions, as a rule, require significant time and resources. At the same time, there are multiple shortcomings. First, this practice introduces serious delays. Second, information about tasks tends to become obsolete, so the longer a decision is made, the less it will be based on reliable data. Third, the significance of these steps is largely exaggerated. And finally, the most unpleasant thing: a long stage of preliminary assessment serves as a catalyst for creating a hybrid model, called Water-scrum-fall: the team believes that it works fashionably and flexibly, while in fact it moves in a very traditional way:

The difficulties of the first step are related to the need to select the task which should be done first from the common pool; for this a set of criteria is often applied. First, it is required to evaluate the potential benefit in one way or another — at least, by comparing this task with the others. Benefits evaluation is not easy: methods like Scrum do not help much in this matter; they expect this information to come from the customer or the product owner. Then there is a desire to estimate the resources required for the task, but it is also difficult, especially for tasks taken for the first time. Techniques such as Planning

---
41 Ries, E., *The Lean Startup*, 2011, ISBN 978-0307887894

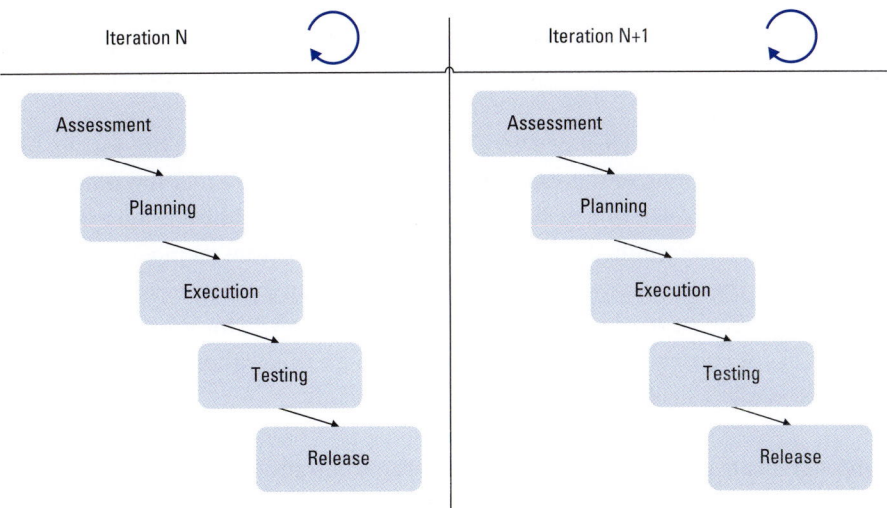

Fig. 4.13   Waterfall, skilfully disguised as iterations

Poker could be mentioned here, but we will not consider them seriously and in detail. Finally, it is very dangerous to remove the urgency from consideration; evaluation of benefits and resources should not be done abstractly, but at a certain context, and the expected return often depends on release date; describing it as ASAP is not sufficient.

In 2009, Don Reinertsen proposed a fundamentally different approach to prioritization, calling it the Cost of Delay[42]. The method is relatively simple; it is based on an economic evaluation of the significance of the decision being made, and works better if the queue of work is large. The first step of the method is to determine the key metric for the given value stream. In many cases, it will predictably be a financial return, but there may be situations where another indicator is more significant. Having defined the measurement unit, for each task one needs to calculate or estimate what will happen to the chosen metric if the task is delayed in the queue. Don Reinertsen's experience shows that many team members do not understand the actual value of this indicator, and all attempts to estimate it, as a rule, give a significant error. Reinertsen insists on the most accurate calculation possible, taking into account the dynamics of the value in time. This approach opens uncomfortable questions, which the team will eventually learn to answer.

Having received the value of the key Cost of Delay metric, it is quite easy to compare different tasks among themselves. In the simplest case, for tasks with the same duration, the one with higher cost of the delay should get in the queue. In a more complex case, it is convenient to use the derived metric: The Cost of Delay Divided by Duration, or CD3. The benefit of taking the duration of task into account is in demonstrating how long tasks block the queue for other smaller tasks, delaying the potential benefit from the latter. So,

---

[42] Reinertsen, D., *The Principles of Product Development Flow: Second Generation Lean Product Development*, 2009, ISBN 978-1935401001

the very principle of prioritization encourages reduction of the batch size, preserving their value, which speeds up the product delivery and ensures a more even workload.

One of the advantages of the Cost of Delay method is that it is easy to use for the one who is at the very beginning of the value stream: it is usually there that the time is lost significantly and the acceleration will have the greatest effect. Indeed, once a single significant indicator is determined for each task, then, once the team member is free, they will simply take on the next task with the highest cost of delay (or CD3) from the queue. The same principle can be used further along the chain, however, for short iterations in one or two weeks at subsequent stages, it is possible to do this without prioritization at all, trusting the earlier calculations.

The second significant advantage of this method is economically sound decision-making, which is transparent for all participants. Bringing together several parameters, waiting for approval by a superior, or using the HiPPO method (see Section 4.4 *Limit the WIP*) is not required.

Finally, the third (and not so obvious) feature of the method is assistance in actively mastering the practice of limiting the WIP. Indeed, if you run several tasks simultaneously, the metric will give the worst cost of the delay, so if you follow the method clearly, no one will ever take several tasks at once.

However, it should be remembered that the cost of delay is not another additional parameter to the already available set. On the contrary, it is designed to exclude all other parameters, simplifying decision making and reducing waste at the very start of the value stream.

4.11 Continual identification, exploitation and elevation of constraints

The value stream discussed in Chapter 3 *The Principles* will always have constraints. They should always be taken into account. The state of an even flow without delays is not achieved overnight and requires effort. And this means the need for the next practice: using visualization tools along with WIP limits, one can identify the bottlenecks of this value stream. Among all the known bottlenecks, there is one that causes the greatest delay — this is the one to focus on.

Actually, work with a bottleneck consists of two steps. First, it is necessary to understand how to change the rules of work short-term, in order to use (exploit) the identified bottleneck to the fullest. For example, to limit tasks in a stream so that they do not overload the bottleneck, and to transfer only high-priority, important tasks to this point. Second, we need to find a way to eliminate the bottleneck, to get rid of it. That said, it is worth remembering the danger of getting a constraint in the same place once again after a while, due to the inertia of the system and the tendency of processes to return to the previous, habitual state.

After eliminating the identified constraint, it is possible to undo previously established short-term rules and to start searching for the next most significant bottleneck.

4.12 Summary

The volume of any book is naturally limited. Moreover, the volume of this book is limited consciously: few people in today's realities have the opportunity to spend a significant amount of time reading long texts. Therefore, review of other DevOps practices (and there are a great many of them in books and in the wild), is left out.

It is worth noting that, as explained in Chapter 2 *The Foundation*, many of DevOps practices are inherited or borrowed from such areas as Theory of Constraints, lean production, continuous deployment and other long-standing areas of management. This, of course, does not make them less useful for solving management problems in DevOps. In the further study of such practices, a lot of interesting, already published books may prove useful for the reader; and the final Chapter 5 of this book is about practical application of DevOps.

5 Practical Application

5.1 DevOps applicability and limitations

Probably, the previous chapter has made to the reader the impression of a fairy tale: it would be great to be in it! The employees in self-organizing teams would be completely motivated. Business and IT would explore together for ways to beloved customers and their money; IT systems would become stable and antifragile; and changes and releases would be flowing steadily, along with decreasing technical debt... The previously chosen method of explanation through comparison of 'traditional' practice with 'DevOps practice' could leave an impression of emphasizing the advantages and concealing the shortcomings.

At the same time, I tried to consider all aspects of DevOps as impartially as possible. As stated at the very beginning of this book, DevOps is one of the tools, albeit new, in the hands of a modern IT manager. Like other management tools, it is not a cure for all diseases, but is best suited for solving specific problems. And, like every tool, it has its limits. Let's take a look at them, still adhering to a sober and pragmatic view.

Since you have reached the last chapter of this book, the life of your IT department is, most likely, arranged quite differently at the moment. The scale of the changes that are required is large, and it is worthwhile to start large transformations only if there is a clear understanding of two aspects: the benefits and the viability. Let us look at them one by one.

To begin with, not every organization should think about DevOps in principle. First, let's exclude special cases: commercial software developers, system integrators, IT outsourcers, and project-oriented organizations. What is common in all these cases is participation only in a limited part of the value stream. See Figure 5.1.

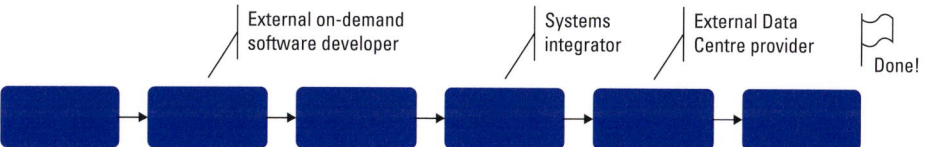

Fig. 5.1 Special cases, not considered below

Applicability of DevOps to such situations is a subject worthy of a separate publication. We will focus on a more traditional layout: a business that has an internal or external IT department that is fully responsible for all information technology matters. Actually, the area of business and the form of ownership of such organizations are not so important:

it can be a bank, an insurance company, a trade organization, a non-profit entity, a production or service business. The main thing is that this organization uses information technologies, and hence the objective is to obtain the maximum return from IT.

Organizations become interested in DevOps when the following conditions are met:
- the core business of the company is highly dependent on information technology (the dependence can be easily assessed by indirect criteria: for example, by the share of IT costs in the organization's budget and the seat of the top IT manager in the company's hierarchy);
- the rate of change occurring in the information technology used by this organization, is high;
- the main business requires rapid changes to test new business ideas or hypotheses (see *Decrease time to market*);
- there are IT-related risks for the core business, which owners or top management consider to be unacceptable;
- all other tried-and-tested methods of increasing effectiveness no longer give significant results.

> Here is an example of the risks mentioned in the list above: One million new customers connect to the Apple Pay system every week[43]. Part of the transaction income from their payments for completely different services, unrelated to Apple products and services, is now received by this corporation, rather than by banks. The scale of losses can be estimated by comparing the total number of active Visa cards (about 2.5 billion) and active iPhone devices (0.7 billion)[44]. A similar story develops at the same time with the Android Pay system. At the same time, neither Apple, nor Google have a banking license, they do not have to comply with strict legislative requirements applied to financial organizations, they do not bear expenses for the maintenance of branches and ATM networks. What they have is a powerful financial resource, advanced technology and access to the loyal customer base, which is unattainable for any financial institution in the world. Moving at the usual fast pace of IT companies, they pose a threat to any unwieldy traditional bank, accustomed for decades to get its income the usual way — from settlement transactions, deposits and loans, like all other banks.

If for the given organization, the conditions in the above list are relevant, the use of DevOps in one form or another has a potential value.

We should separately mention the cases when organizations consider the use of DevOps to drastically reduce the accumulated technical debt, or to eliminate fragility of the IT infrastructure. It should be remembered that for complex situations being carried away

---

43 http://fortune.com/2017/05/02/apple-pay-volume-up/
44 http://fortune.com/2017/03/06/apple-iphone-use-worldwide/

by DevOps most likely will not bring much profit and will definitely give no quick wins; on the contrary, organizational and technology changes can lead to chaos and loss of control. Chronic problems should be solved carefully, thoughtfully and judiciously, not hoping that DevOps is a magical cure for all diseases.

Let's move on to the second aspect, viability. Can DevOps be 'built' in all organizations? Many experts are inclined to a positive response. As confirmation, there is a case of the HP LaserJet Firmware division. There are more than 400 developers of firmware for printers, scanners and multifunctional devices in this department, with employees in three countries. In the initial state, only a small portion of the marketing department's requests for development were accepted; releases were made every 6 months; and only 5% of the employees' working hours were spent on developing new functionality. Over the course of four years it was possible to accelerate the development of up to 10-15 assemblies daily, increase employees' productivity by up to 40%, reduce testing time from three weeks to one day, and other miracles.

The above example, for all its reality, lies outside the previously outlined area of 'business that has its own IT department'. It can be used as an didactical story, but does not help to identify the limitations of the applicability of DevOps. However, the list of main challenges is finite and, on the whole, it is quite clear.

DevOps is not very suitable for those who do not have their own software development: for example when all the core software in use is commercial off-the shelf (COTS), and is configured via user or admin interface. If the company has no in-house software development, there is no start of the value stream; there is no possibility to control the versions of the source code (since there is no access to the source code and there are no competences to understand it). But there is a significant dependency on the vendor and supplier of the software. The negative consequences of this dependency are well known: no matter how large and well-known your organization is, you will usually be only one of many customers, and despite all the assurances of vendor's account managers, you will be in the same queue waiting for developer's attention, as all the others. What is important here is not your number in the queue, but the very fact of its existence. Another negative consequence of the dependency on the external software is the extreme tardiness of many software vendors due to the use of those waterfall models and long release cycles. There are cases when critical errors in a new version of the software remain uncorrected for more than nine months, individual failures are not diagnosed for more than half a year and the client is offered a bleak choice: either to stay for another two or three years with the old version that has long-term support (LTS) and seems to have fewer defects; or constantly switch to every new version, where some old errors are fixed, and some new introduced. Work in such situations will be discussed in more detail in the *COTS* section below.

Another challenge of DevOps implementation will arise in organizations using their own software, where developers are not members of staff: development is carried out by other companies to order, or developers work under some sort of a contract: freelance, outstaffing or the like. In this case, it is difficult to fully include them in the value stream because of the completely different motivation. Full-time employees are usually more interested in meeting the needs of the core business, in the company's prosperity, in their own career growth, and therefore in the high-quality final product of their work. External developers are more likely to limit their liability in a strict accordance to the contract and to focus on formal fulfilment of the work order, sometimes overstating the workload and time. We should also add to consideration the possible frequent change of employees, their partial allocation to the given team, as well as the typical situation where agreement on the scope and terms of engagement is made by certain parties (say, the head of the business development from the consumer's side and the account manager from the contractor's side), while ongoing interactions are performed by some other parties (external developers and the rest of the customers' IT team). In this case, many of the principles outlined in Section 4.2 *Unusual teams*, become impossible or distorted. We should note that, while five years ago it was very trendy to outsource nearly everything, apart from the core business processes, nowadays there is a tendency to return in-house software development and IT operations back into the company. It is considered rather stupid not to do this when competition in various industries boils down to competition in application of software-based information technologies.

> *In short, software is eating the world.*
>
> *More and more major businesses and industries are being run on software and delivered as online services — from movies to agriculture to national defense. Many of the winners are Silicon Valley-style entrepreneurial technology companies that are invading and overturning established industry structures. Over the next 10 years, I expect many more industries to be disrupted by software, with new world-beating Silicon Valley companies doing the disruption in more cases than not.*[45]
>
> Marc Andreessen,
> co-founder of Netscape,
> co-founder and partner of the venture fund Andreessen-Horowitz, 2011

The next constraint of the implementation of DevOps are long-standing, established processes, backed by a decision hierarchy, organizational structure, internal regulatory documentation, bureaucracy and corporate culture. Some large organizations make a sober estimate of their ability to change as limited, while the transition to DevOps requires a major restructuring not only of the IT department, but also of the business units. Suffice

---

[45] https://a16z.com/2016/08/20/why-software-is-eating-the-world/

it to recall the differences between the culture of traditional large corporations and the culture of startups, listed in Section 4.1.7 *Act as a startup*, in order to understand the scale of the transformation required. It is important to note that for many organizations, a complete change in the existing work practices is fundamentally impossible, despite the demonstrated short-term success in some parts of the organization.

Finally, the last significant obstacle is the monolithic, rigidly bound IT architecture. Introduction of small teams requires the ability to assign a separate area of responsibility to each of them. In a situation where the IT system in question is still being developed and maintained by dozens or hundreds of employees as a single entity, it will be difficult to separate parts for individual independent teams that work asynchronously. Some thoughts on this issue are given below in Section 5.3 *Evolving architecture*.

To the above complications, we need to add a few more factors that limit the use of DevOps, in the opinion of many. But first we should note that these factors are incorrectly viewed as problems that shut the door on DevOps initiatives. It is more correct to treat them as constraints that can be eliminated, that is, as tasks that do have solutions:

- Lack of readiness to create DevOps teams, as described above. For example, some organizations encourage their employees to work remotely without having to be in the office at certain hours. This is the case in geographically distributed companies, where employees of IT departments are not all in one place. Finally, in many organizations the organizational structure is so rigid that it does not cater for creating cross-functional teams. All these examples illustrate the above thesis: they are not a stop factor on the way to DevOps, they only require appropriate changes, corrections, which may not be easy, but are nevertheless possible.
- 'Special' requirements to information security or regulatory compliance. The word 'special' is intentionally in quotation marks: a more careful consideration of the matter in a particular company can show that in reality this organization does not fundamentally differ from the others operating in the same industry. Yes, compliance requirements or information security requirements should be taken into account; however, it is more a question of approach and technology, rather than the need to work in an exclusively conventional way.
- Minimal use of virtualization and cloud computing, or the abandonment of these technologies altogether, as well as the use of highly outdated programming languages. The points given in the first part of the book, show the need for using cloud computing. As it was shown in Section 1.1 *Origins*, it was due to them that DevOps became possible. Companies that have limited use of virtualization will have certain difficulties implementing DevOps. However, the choice of a particular technology is a decision of each company, and if new management tools require the use of new information technologies, the relevant changes can be planned and implemented.

The following illustration summarizes all the main driving motivations towards DevOps, as well as factors limiting the use of DevOps:

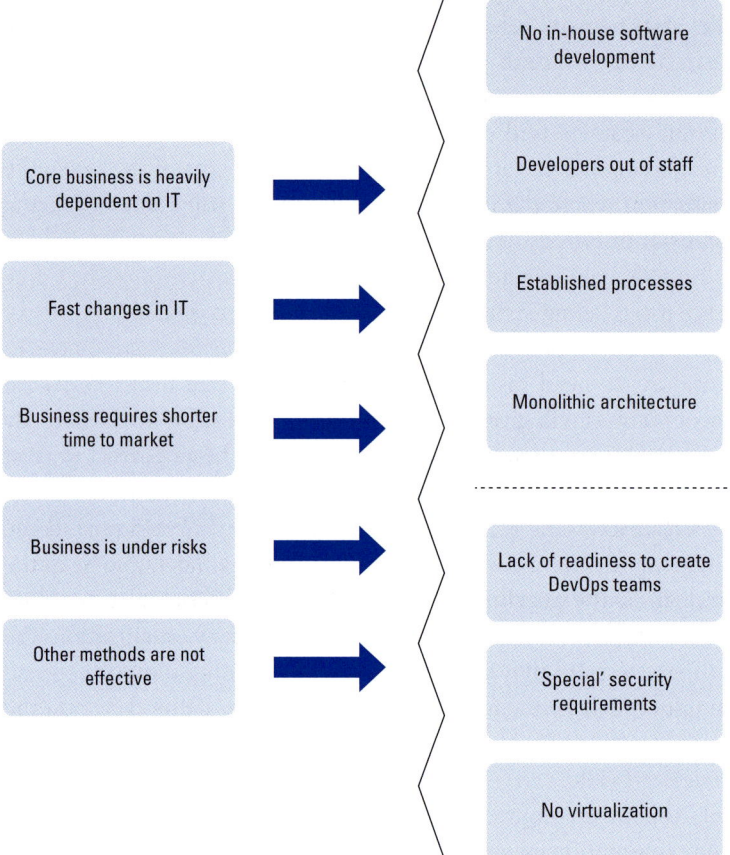

Fig. 5.2   Interest in DevOps and known constraints

Obviously, the presence of one of these limiting factors does not make DevOps impossible for this company. Some benefits can be obtained in difficult conditions, and many restrictions can be circumvented in one way or another. It is also obvious that the set of limiting factors further complicates the use of DevOps. When that limit comes, where the restrictions form an insurmountable barrier (and whether it comes at all), is unknown. However, HP's example of firmware development, like the existing examples of DevOps implementation on mainframe architecture, shows that it is likely that the limit is much further away than is commonly thought.

5.2 COTS

Striving to save on information technologies, to reduce the complexity of systems and to get the return quicker, many organizations follow the principle *To minimize in-house software development and to buy as much as possible ready-made software*. The class of ready-to-use software even has its own name: COTS (Commercial Off-the-Shelf). This approach is quite common and for good reason. However, as shown above, the use of COTS can become a serious obstacle for the application of DevOps. Faced with the problem of 'compatibility' of DevOps and COTS, organizations have developed the following set of recommendations.

First, do not use COTS to automate strategic business lines. In a situation where competition shifts towards information and information technology, it is necessary to have maximum flexibility and control, usually unattainable with COTS. Therefore, the first advice that any serious expert will give you is to get rid of the COTS working in the most important areas of your business; move to in-house software development.

If the use of COTS, albeit temporary, is inevitable, then specific applications and the strategy of managing them should be chosen with the following classification in mind:
- open applications, such as Salesforce, allow you to use standard functionality, adapting it to your business processes;
- closed applications, such as Adobe products, do not really imply any adaption;
- platform applications, such as Microsoft Dynamics, are the foundation for building your own IT systems.

With COTS, it is necessary to follow the same principles as with in-house software within the scope of DevOps practices. Get rid of the installation and configuration through user or admin interfaces; instead, you will have to study the installation process in detail, understand what the installer does, what files are created and changed, what modifications are made to databases, and so on. Next, create your own script, replicating the work of the original installer[46]. You may need to develop several scripts to installing and configuring the system in different environments being used or planned: testing, acceptance, or production. All scripts should be stored in the version control system. If necessary, application libraries, binary and other supporting files can be stored in the same system, or in the artifact storage system. the essence is to get rid of the manual and complicated installation and configuration process, replacing it with automated deployment performed by known and controlled scripts.

---

46 It's worth mentioning how enthusiasts keep creating so-called portable versions of some popular applications, without any access to the source code or knowledge of the internal architecture of these applications. Portable versions can be launched and fully used without installation at the target computer. If enthusiasts can do this kind of work, sometimes for rather complex applications, this opportunity can also be considered for industrial systems.

Similarly, it's advised to reconsider the approach to the setup of the software in operation. Automated control systems allow to identify areas that almost never change when application is configured and updated. And vice versa, configuration items and files that change by nearly every configuration, which means they are subject to rigorous control in the version control system. The ultimate task is to have a separately stored full copy of all application settings under version control at any given time.

At the very least, the following solutions are possible:
1. Standard configuration tools for COTS, such as the IDE (Integrated Development Environment), incorporate system configuration change hooks. As soon as the administrator or developer changes something in the application, the hook detects the changes made, converts them into a format suitable for the version control system and sends the end file or files to it; in some cases, checking for conflicts between changes. Later, using the built-in mechanisms for configurations import, it is possible to change or restore the system settings without using the IDE. This type of configuration control is the least expensive, but it is not supported by all IT systems.
2. Application settings are exported in a format suitable for the version control system. Ideally, this export is done automatically, triggered by changes in the COTS. If there is no trigger, the export is scheduled to match the flow of changes in the system (for example, every night). As a rule, version control systems allow comparing incoming files with the stored ones, and if there are no changes, the tracking load is insignificant, and the information is not duplicated. This method is more expensive than the first one, but it is more universal.
3. The most expensive method works for cases where COTS does not support configuration export, but has some import capabilities. It is to develop your own COTS configuration application. All configurations are done in this application; configuration files in the required format are stored in the version control system and imported into the target IT system in the COTS format.

In fact, it's about recreating a fragment of the development environment for an application with unavailable source code. However, the work does not end there. It is necessary to develop tests that can be run automatically, checking the introduced changes; overall system operations; integration and interactions with other systems. Automated testing is a part of the deployment pipeline, which should work for COTS as well.

The best-case scenario for COTS is a regular rapid automated full re-creation of the application in the production environment from scratch, based on the data of the configuration management system, without system downtime and unnoticed by users. Such level of control ensures that there are no surprises when changes are made to the systems and that unsuccessful changes are rolled back early and automatically.

5.3 Evolving architecture

Earlier, in Section 5.1 *DevOps applicability and limitations*, we highlighted the challenge faced by many organizations formed before 2010: a monolithic IT architecture with tight connections between system components. Modern applications consist of a set of interacting objects: interconnected structures are created at the level of business logic, data, IT infrastructure and others. Systems are designed and developed as a single entity, both horizontally (objects and communications between them) and vertically (applications, servers, DBMS, protocols and interfaces for data exchange). A whole set of difficulties comes with this architecture:
- even small changes in one part of the system can lead to negative, often unpredictable effects in other parts;
- many developers work simultaneously on the functionality of the system, each on their own part, which requires resources for the coordination;
- very few employees understand the IT system landscape holistically, with all dependencies and constraints; these employees quickly become very valuable, irreplaceable and overloaded;
- any documentation on the IT system quickly becomes obsolete;
- IT system's development and operation are separated in a natural way: operations and support staff do not get into complex details of the system architecture, and therefore they have to escalate even relatively simple questions to developers;
- it is difficult to identify responsibility areas for small self-sufficient teams, so the main advantages of agile development are reduced to none and do not meet expectations;
- the existing architecture does not fully address current requirements, it becomes obsolete soon after it is created: key architecture decisions were made when there was not enough information, there was no experience in developing and using the system, and life had not taken its course yet;
- changing and developing the architecture itself is not easy due to the large number of rigid links.

The traditional answer to these challenges is in some formal management processes and increase in the number of controls, and it slows down the changes. For example, changing a line of code to fix an error may take several minutes for the developer, followed by several months of formalities before it goes to the production environment. The system should be tested as a whole, with the integration of multiple changes made by many developers. To cope with it, IT departments introduce additional artificial barriers also known as release calendar. Indeed, if testing of the changes is complicated and requires significant resources, then it should be done as rarely as possible. Unfortunately, this approach, however rigorous, does not prevent defects from appearing in a production environment.

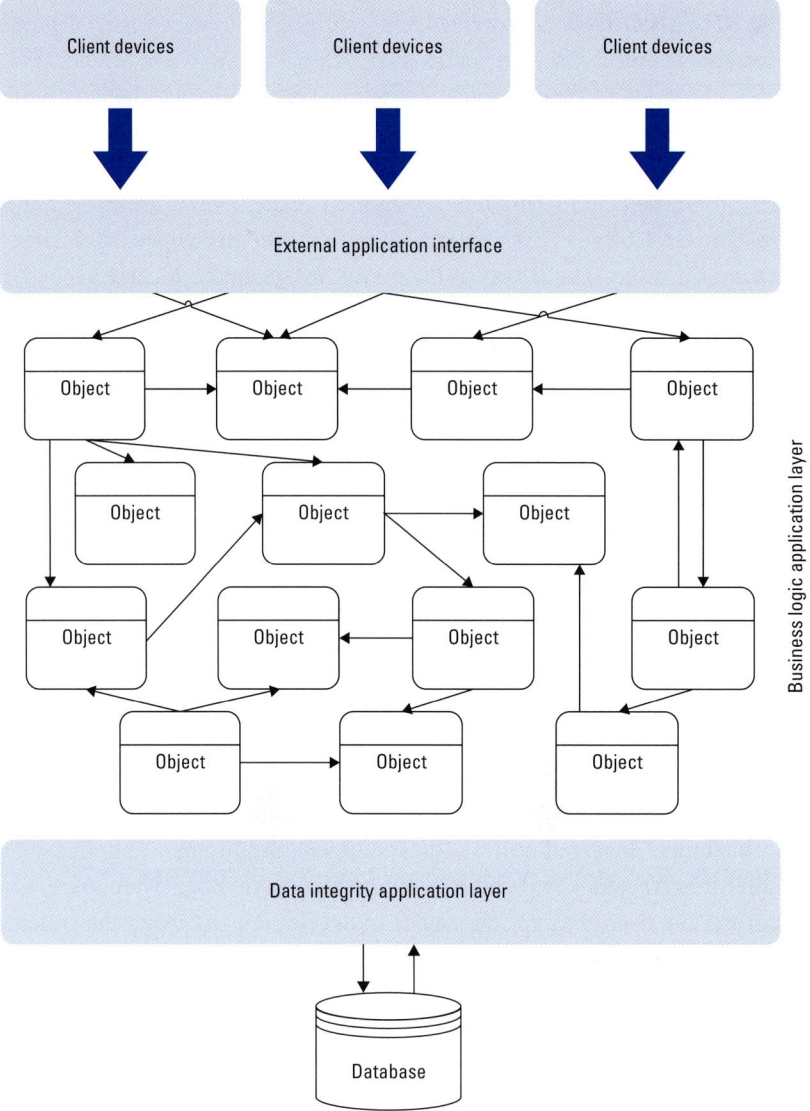

Fig. 5.3   Illustrative monolithic architecture of a very simple IT system (not all links are shown)

These problems of the monolithic architecture manifested a long time ago, when first experience in the operation and development of large information systems was gained. Engineers are constantly on the hunt for better ideas: modular architectures, microkernel architecture, event-driven architecture (using brokers or mediators), service-oriented architecture (SOA), and others, including hybrid ones based on the listed above. However, as the authors of *Building Evolutionary Architectures*[47] note, they all have significant drawbacks and sometimes higher level of complexity, which makes them poorly applicable to DevOps initiatives.

---

47   Ford, N., R. Parsons, P. Kua, *Building Evolutionary Architectures*, 2017, ISBN 978-1-491-98636-3.

A radical, promising solution that has received much attention in recent years, is the so-called microservice architecture. Applications are designed as a set of domain-based elements: each of them is 'responsible' for the specific essence of the IT system and includes all the necessary technical and infrastructure components on which, for example, databases and libraries depend. Such services are not *connected* with each other; instead, they *communicate* exclusively through the specified program interfaces or message queues. None of the services should know about the internal arrangement of other services or have any dependencies on it. The *Share Nothing* principle is used.

Following the above recommendations, it is possible to achieve a state where modification of any of the services can be done independently of others, and by a dedicated team. Working with each of the services separately and with the IT system as a whole, it becomes possible to follow all the basic DevOps principles: the value stream, the deployment pipeline, keeping everything in the version control system, automated configuration management, and Definition of Done. Release calendars and associated months-long waiting are no longer required, and the change management process can be greatly simplified.

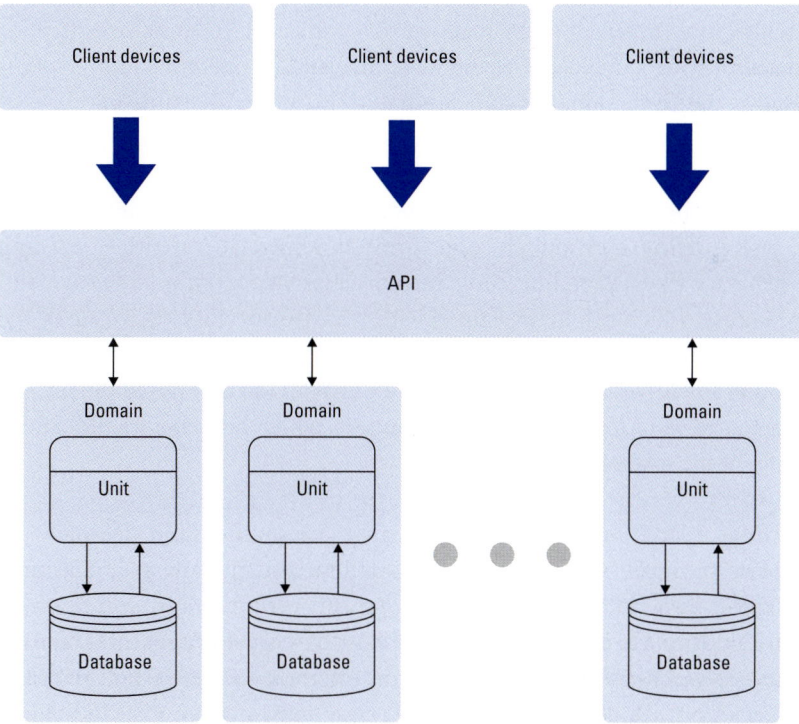

Fig. 5.4   Example of a microservice architecture of a simple IT system (not all domains are shown)

Another great opportunity is moving to an evolving architecture: constantly following new business requirements and emerging technological novelties. For example, a team responsible for domain A can prepare a new version of the functionality without disabling the current version. Service B, which uses the old version of Service A, will continue doing this without loss of quality. At the same time, Service C, designed for a new version of Service A, can access it for new functionality. Gradually, the whole application will be updated to work with the improved version of the domain A, and the previous version can be disabled. And it does not require waiting for all components to be ready for a large-scale overnight migration. Exactly the same way, independently of other teams and domains, one can perform refactoring of individual services, reducing the accumulated technical debt.

Certainly, microservice architecture entails a number of challenges. Domain allocation requires serious study and can hardly be done once and for all: service structure of the system should be reviewed and updated continually. It is necessary to follow clear rules for defining and documenting of interfaces and versions. Ensuring integrity of the data references is shifting significantly: from the database management system level to the domain level. It will be necessary to monitor each of the services: not only for operations control, but also to track usage.

The introduction of containerization has contributed significantly to the expansion of microservice architectures in recent years. It allows to organize an isolated workspace for a service without allocating a dedicated virtual machine; and all operations for creation and management of the containers are software-based, including dynamic addition of capacity as demand increases and the same automatic resource release when it decreases.

However, for most organizations, transition to microservices is far from simple. Some companies allocate funding and launch large projects aimed at 'rewriting' existing information systems for the new architecture. Such projects take months and years, and as a rule, to no success, which can be explained with two reasons. First, the scale of the transformations is so large that it is impossible to complete the work in a reasonable time, even if all other initiatives are frozen. Second, along with the new development, the system continues to evolve in response to business needs, which brings more difficulties to synchronization of the systems functionality.

Instead of launching a large project with little chance for success (and definitely no quick wins), experts recommend[48] to manage the architecture upgrade as a continual activity and to treat it as part of the regular development work. Dealing with the next business request, it's possible to allocate a part of the existing system to a separate domain supported by the necessary environment: a program interface for interaction with the main system; a set of tests, a deployment pipeline. Gradually, step by step, individual parts of the monolithic system will be implemented in the microservice architecture, with business requirements as the main driver of changes.

---

48 Humble, J., J. Molesky, B. O'Reilly, *Lean Enterprise: How High Performance Organizations Innovate at Scale*, 2015, ISBN 978-1449368425

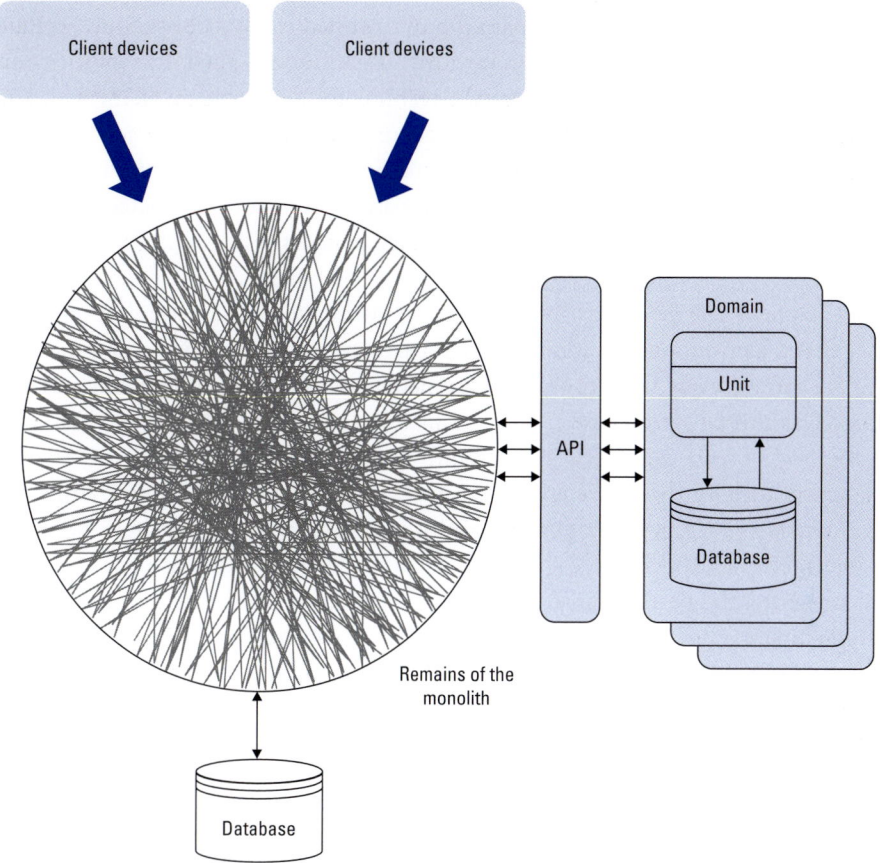

Fig. 5.5   Gradual transition to microservice architecture for an existing application system

5.4   DevOps and ITSM

Myth: DevOps is incompatible with ITIL®

DevOps practices can be made compatible with ITIL process. However, to support the shorter lead times and higher deployment frequencies associated with DevOps, many areas of the ITIL processes become fully automated, solving many problems associated with the configuration and release management processes. And because DevOps requires fast detection and recovery when service incidents occur, the ITIL disciplines of service design, incident, and problem management remain as relevant as ever.

The DevOps Handbook[49]

---

49 Kim, G., J. Humble, P. Debois, J. Willis, *The Devops Handbook: How to Create Worldclass Agility, Reliability and Security in Technology Organizations*, 2016, ISBN 978-1-942-78800-3

Over the past twenty years, many companies have invested millions of pounds, dollars and euros in ITIL®. The spendings are justified: organizations look for solutions to management problems related to information technology, and struggle to improve the effectiveness of IT departments. In the field of corporate IT management, such bodies of knowledge as ITIL® and COBIT are generally recognized industry standards, although it is not entirely correct to use the term *standard* here. Many companies expected to benefit from ITIL®; they have received and are receiving such benefits.

However, Chapter 3 *The Principles* and Chapter 4 *Key Practices* have a number of theses and cases that a conventional, traditional IT department cannot accept easily; the new practices are too far away from those that are being used in the vast majority of large companies. Can this be a problem?

DevOps experts believe that there are no fundamental difficulties. The quote from *The DevOps Handbook* given at the beginning of this section is a typical example. Some IT service management experts are even more encouraged by new perspectives and are urgently mastering the new religion. Presentations and even whole sections devoted to DevOps and digital transformation were seen at many ITSM conferences in 2017. It seems that almost all experts unanimously believe that ITIL-based processes can be somehow adapted for, or aligned with DevOps, while preserving the investments. However, it's not that simple.

There is a fundamental contradiction between DevOps ideas and those of ITSM, which needs to be resolved. One of the two key principles of IT service management (along with process-based approach to management of activities) is delivery of business value from IT in the form of services. An integral part of service approach is the customer-to-supplier relationships: the first determines what and why is needed, the second takes on (some) risks and costs associated with the achievement. These relationships are expected to be documented in detail in a service level agreement (SLA), with respective responsibilities of the parties. If the customer is not satisfied with the quality of the services delivered, they can try to influence the service provider appealing to the signed agreement, or even change the provider. Likewise, if the supplier finds that the customer causes more difficulties than the profit, they can terminate the agreement and focus on other customers. Of course, the situation is not that simple for providers internal to their customers, but the basic principle remains the same.

At the same time, DevOps is in the most significant degree based on the concept of a single team, which includes IT and business. Working together, they are more focused on the long-term victories, rather than on short-term wins, and certainly not on observing formal agreements. Together, they walk along the road, which becomes clearly visible only as they move forward. They agreed that in case of failures they would not look for the guilty, but learn from their own mistakes. In the extreme case, the border between IT and business disappears altogether, which is completely different from the 'us and them' approach described above.

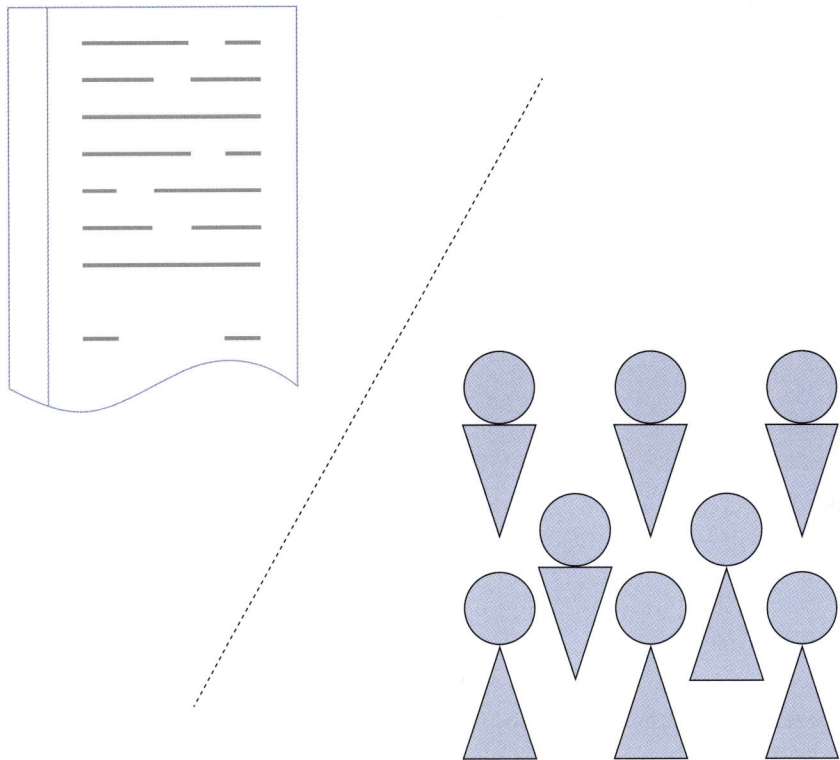

Fig. 5.6   The essence of ITSM and the essence of DevOps

The answer to this major contradiction has yet to be found, but there are also some discrepancies in small things, relatively speaking. For example:
- As mentioned above, DevOps practices differ in many respects from the customary practices of a traditional IT department — and many IT managers are not ready to accept the new ideas.
- Funding in DevOps is organized in a completely different way: funds are allocated to products, rather than projects.
- For many years, companies have worked with the IT department on the principle of optimization for costs; DevOps suggests switching to optimization for speed.
- Change management 'according to ITIL®' is focused on mitigating the risks; It is achieved by a relatively slow and strictly formalized process with a lot of controls, notifications, agreements and approvals. Changes 'according to DevOps' should be made as quickly as possible, with proper automated testing and logging.
- Configuration management and Configuration Management Database (as described in ITIL®) are hard to find in real life due to the excessive laboriousness and abundance of manual operations needed to collect and update configuration information. At the

same time, configuration management in DevOps is performed to a significant degree automatically and on a mandatory basis, so much so that the actual term *configuration* gets a new meaning.
- The concept of *release* changes: from "release is a complex of changes prepared, tested and executed simultaneously" to "new functionality available to customers".
- Incident management practices, including segregation of support lines and functional escalation, are replaced by another principle: *You build it, you run it.*
- Problem management (dealing with root causes of incidents) does not make sense: it is difficult to organize it in ITSM and it is not necessary in DevOps.
- ITIL® capacity management is to a great extend based on a capacity plan, which should cover all demand for IT resource, and is tied to the company's budgeting cycle, usually annual. In DevOps, capacity must be available at the moment it is required, without delays for finding a supplier, signing a contract, waiting for the delivery, etc.

And so on. It turns out, wherever you look, ITIL® recommendations differ from the ideas and practices of DevOps. Perhaps, these discrepancies are insignificant and only light adjustment of existing ITSM processes are needed; however, the more likely is a scenario where ITIL® processes are changed beyond recognition.

5.5   Cargo culting

A huge number of teams seeking to master new management practices do not give due attention to *management*, focusing on *practices* only. Iterative development is fashionable now? Okay, we will arrange two-week sprints. Everyone around holds daily Scrum stand-ups? Excellent, we have them now. They say that Kanban boards make sense? Fine, we will get a Kanban. A DevOps pipeline cannot work without automation? Well, we will ask the guys to select and implement some systems. And so on.

This behavior where the emphasis shifts towards rituals instead of goals, meaning and principles, is called the cargo cult. The concept was first applied in 1945 in an area that has nothing to do with information technology: anthropology. Scientists, who studied the customs and traditions of Papua New Guinea, identified and described the phenomenon in which, according to aboriginal people, the availability of material and spiritual benefits depends more on the will of spirits and gods. To obtain such benefits, one needs to perform certain actions and rites, as a rule — under the guidance of a shaman or an elder. Examples and confirmations of the cargo cult were discovered earlier; the oldest was documented in 1885 on the Fiji Islands. Occasional evidences of the cult have survived in some parts of Oceania till now.

The most striking and best-known example of the cargo cult is the story that occurred during and immediately after the Second World War on the islands of Melanesia, which were strategically important for combat operations. First, the Japanese air forces landed on the islands, bringing with them unprecedented goods, clothing, medicines, food, and weapons, etc. Then the islands came under control of the anti-Hitler coalition; one way or another, the local population firmly linked the appearance of useful goods that never could be produced locally, with white people coming from the sky. Shortly after the end of the war, the islands lost their importance, military bases were curtailed, and foreigners left the territory. Looking for a way to restore the flow of goods, the aborigine people engaged in the most accurate reproduction of all those conditions under which the treasure used to literally come from the sky. Namely, they began to decorate themselves in the colours of the American army, to do military marches on the parade ground, to produce rifles of bamboo, and to copy all other external features of the recent past. It came to constructing buildings that copied command posts of airfields, including interior equipment and aerials — made, however, all the same from bamboo. Additional grounds in the jungle were cleared to create more 'airfields'; they were fitted with fairly accurate copies of the aircrafts. Of course, all these actions did not lead to the return of foreigners, or to receiving new goods.

Fig. 5.7   A modern bamboo computer that allows virtualization

Any educated person understands that this story could not end otherwise — it is not enough to copy someone else's activities in order to get the same products. However, what is obvious in the example with aborigines is often completely omitted in everyday business situations. Thoughtless copying of agile software development rituals in the hope to accelerate the products launch can be found in the practice of various companies more often than it should.

It is notable that the cargo cult phenomenon can be observed in IT service management as often as in DevOps. Unfortunately, there is not enough information to analyse the regularities yet.

5.6 Start where you are, progress iteratively

> — What would you recommend IT managers should do with DevOps?
> — Start now! Today is the best day to start.
> Interview with Gary Gruver, the manager who changed HP LaserJet Firmware Division forever[50], 2017

Previous sections of the book were supposed to create a sense of scale of the change to the reader: the use of DevOps implies new management principles, new approaches to dealing with information technology. Many know from their own experience that big transformations are never easy. Even when IT infrastructure is hard to manage, business managers keep asking inconvenient questions about the time to market, and constant pressure is experienced from all directions, managers still do their best to stay in the zone of relative comfort, where things are more or less clear and predictable, albeit not as beautiful as they would like. The large scale of changes should not confuse and stop you: it is not 'All or nothing'.

If you find yourself in the situation described in Section 5.1 *DevOps applicability and limitations*, then there is really no reason to wait. DevOps movement is at the beginning of its journey. Of course: there are still many open questions, especially in the field of corporate information technologies. Is it worth waiting for someone to find all the answers? By no means! As described at the very beginning of the book, the pioneers may not be doing the best job, but they accumulate their own experience, and it allows them to move forward faster than the ones behind. Currently, there are so many publications, events and evangelists in DevOps space, that information vacuum is simply impossible. On the contrary, filtering information from the noise is more and more important. What is published does not necessarily correspond to reality; marketing hype hides real difficulties and failures; and everyone can suddenly become an 'expert' nowadays. This is why making up your own view on the subject area, raising your own questions and finding answers, is more important than ever.

As with IT service management, the common mistake is an attempt to *implement* DevOps. Of course, you cannot implement DevOps, this phrase has no more meaning than 'to implement a healthy diet' or 'to implement a hammer'. DevOps can be used, utilized like any other management tool, to solve specific problems of the organization. DevOps is not a software product that can be installed and started, nor an engineer that can be hired to bring the new order to IT. In many ways DevOps requires cultural and organizational changes, and these changes are not limited to the IT department.

---

[50] https://cleverics.ru/subject-field/interviews/723-gary-gruver-interview-on-devops

Business units will also have to change, exactly in the same key areas as the IT department: organizationally, culturally and instrumentally. It is naive to believe that an IT department following the new principles can interact with the business units in the old way. On the contrary, DevOps implies that not only the boundary between development and operation would disappear, but also between IT and business. If this target state is far away, at least, new ways of interaction and new funding principles for IT are required. Such changes are impossible without strong and unconditional support at the highest level of organization. *"You have my full commitment, apart from time, money, effort, and just so long as I don't have to be involved"* is certainly not an option.

DevOps application should in no case be approached as a project. Project approach implies obtaining a unique result within a limited timeframe and a specified budget, while DevOps means playing a long game, from today till forever. Therefore, there is no more meaningless word combination than *DevOps implementation project*.

It is necessary to keep training the staff. Not to train, but to keep training; moreover, it is necessary to create effective environment for sharing knowledge and lessons learned. These mechanisms should be constantly tested. Those that are established in the company and actively used by specialists, should be further developed. Those that do not work, should be removed and replaced by the new ones. Imbalance (for example, towards technical studies of deployment pipeline) should be prevented. It is easy not to see the woods for the trees; a pipeline built in just one part of an organization will not give the expected benefits. We should pay attention to study of the DevOps principles and philosophy, creating a new culture of operation and management of IT.

As with other organizational changes, people will react in different ways: some will welcome changes and make extra efforts, some will be neutral or suspicious, and others will actively oppose, or sabotage the moving forward of the change. In this respect, DevOps is not different from other organizational changes, for which managers have accumulated a sufficient amount of techniques.

A common approach in organizations with legacy IT infrastructure is to identify those systems that are loosely connected with others (these are usually modern 'digital' applications). Use these systems as a pilot: they are usually easier to apply the basic DevOps elements, including value stream, deployment pipeline, version control system, automated configuration management, and so on. This experience can be then applied to other systems, but do not expect it to be easy. Unfortunately, all IT systems are special in their own way, as well as IT teams and business units. Nevertheless, starting with simpler cases, you can move on with more confidence.

It is easy to explain to yourself and to others, why you should not deal with a new subject, or why the new practices will not work and will not take root. This is a well-known cognitive trap, which can only be circumvented by actions.

> Kelsey Hightower, staff developer advocate at Google Cloud Platform, speaks quite categorically[51]:
>
> "There is nothing to figure out in that domain. (...) For me, that is the table stakes. CI/CD, DevOps; we have to say, listen, figure it out, or go work with another team outside this company to figure it out."

5.7 Value stream as the core

Suppose that in an organization a small and well-controlled pilot area is defined. There is a plan to change the way IT is operated and managed in this area to get more benefits: to release new products quicker, to test business ideas quicker, to introduce anti-fragility and to control the technical debt. What exactly should be done first?

Those who have already been down this road, advise to start with the team. The closer it will be to the *Unusual teams* described in Section 4.2, the higher the chances for success.

Then you should map the 'as is' value stream. This exercise will help to create a common, shared understanding of the current process, and then to identify its bottlenecks and to search for waste. Even before proceeding to the next steps, you can try to change the flow so that there is less waste. It is also possible to make a list of hypotheses to be verified about areas, delays and actions that create the maximum waste. This list will come in handy later, as a basis for future improvements.

Now it's time to proceed to building the deployment pipeline for the part of the stream that can be automated. It is not necessary to plan the total automation from the Day One; a basic pipeline that performs at least assembly and initial testing is enough for the start. The first experience of using the pipeline will show the direction for development. Keeping in mind that resources are limited, one should not immediately set yourself high-scale objectives and strive for some unattainable ideal.

It is much more important to enable measurements of the key indicators in the value stream. For each stage of the stream one can come up with a lot, but there is no objective to maximize the number of metrics. At first, you can manage the three most important ones: lead time, process time and the percentage of work done without errors. Constant

---

[51] http://www.zdnet.com/article/time-to-move-on-from-devops-and-continuous-delivery-says-google-executive/

monitoring of these key indicators will prompt areas where improvements would make the most significant effect.

Having understood and found the areas for improvement, it is possible to develop the to-be version of the stream, and to prepare a list of the changes required. Work improvements should be treated not as one-time events, but as permanent work: it should become a common practice to regularly, actively and methodically look for the waste and eliminate it. This is a daily task of everyone in the team.

To remove constraints and minimize waste, one can select those tools from the arsenal of DevOps, lean production and agile software development, which will best serve the task. Thus, the people's behavior is not determined by book practices; it is the analysis of the value stream that sets objectives and helps to select the most appropriate tools and practices.

Then the cycle closes: after implementing the planned changes, it is necessary to understand whether the expected improvements have been realized, what are the key indicators values; where the next bottleneck is and what can be done to remove it. As it has been said many times, the main thing is to get on this road and start moving along it, but it does not have an end point.

Some teams give an example when the target, final to-be state of the stream, is developed at an early stage, and then systematic and gradual movement towards this state begins. This way seems more complicated and risky, since the probability of making mistakes at an early stage is higher. Moreover, there may be no need to define the final state from the beginning; its definition can be subject to constant experimenting.

Once a value stream in the pilot area is built, the next logical step is to expand the experience and practices to other areas. This approach is possible, but the most interesting and complex tasks begin when several DevOps teams that work separately, need to be combined into something bigger, or when several dozen people are involved in DevOps practice of the organization. However, the question of scaling DevOps to large organizations is a separate and significant field of knowledge, which goes beyond the scope of this book.

5.8 Summary

An impartial review of a subject requires an objective representation of its essence, features, advantages and constraints. The least desirable situation is when the reader has a distorted view of DevOps as the best means of solving all issues faced by a modern IT management. This chapter on DevOps application turned out to be unexpectedly voluminous, while the answers to uncomfortable questions about such things as COTS, monolithic architecture, and service approach are still not obvious.

However, one thing is clear enough: it is up to you, whether you will look for answers by yourself, or wait for someone to tell you about their great achievements. 'Their' is the keyword here. In order to make your own achievements, one has to act, not wait.

6   Conclusion

DevOps has its origins and prerequisites for its existence. By 2010, certain conditions developed that formed both a need and a possibility to manage the development and operation of information technologies in a different way. This led to the emergence of the DevOps movement.

DevOps is not a cure for all diseases, in the way that it is often presented by various evangelists. Basically, it helps to solve three pressing and complex problems: reduce time to market, decrease technical debt and eliminate the fragility of information systems.

DevOps stands on a strong foundation of lean production and agile software development. However, it's incorrect to say that DevOps is just the use of already known ideas; on the contrary, not only DevOps extends the mentioned foundation, but it also introduces several important new principles.

Based on these principles, one can seek, invent and apply practices. Many of them may be unusual for IT departments that work in a traditional way, but each of the practices has a good reason behind it, and sometimes an impartial, almost cynical analysis.

One or two years ago, one could argue about what DevOps is and what it is not; what it means; why all this is necessary and what it consists of. However, the picture has become very clear by 2018. Companies established in the last five years, no longer imagine working in a different way; DevOps is a natural part of the corporate culture for them, even if the word itself is not declared every minute and not placed on the banner. Traditional companies with legacy IT solutions, IT processes and IT people are limited in flexibility, but actively look at the new fashionable subject, take the first steps, experiment, make mistakes, and learn. Some of them show stunning achievements, others make plans and cherish hopes. The largest number of the open questions, which are yet to be answered, is related to corporate information technologies. If the technical issues (such as deployment pipeline implementation) are more or less clear, the key problem is: How to get management benefits from DevOps in traditional companies?

The years to follow will be the era of Enterprise DevOps. It will be interesting years; we have a lot to learn.

"Always take on new challenges—even if you are not sure you are completely ready."

Sheryl Sandberg, COO of Facebook

It is possible that, after closing this book, the reader will think: *"Well, it is not a bad book, everything looks clear, but I knew it all before"*. This would be the best compliment to the author: my attempt of a structured, logical, convincing, and as far as possible impartial presentation of a rather difficult subject has borne fruit.

Appendices

Appendix 1 Test: Are you doing DevOps?

For every established area of management, some sort of a measurement appears over time, often called a maturity level. According to predefined criteria, some organizations may try to assess the evidences of various recommended practices in order to derive an integral assessment on an arbitrary scale: to what extent are some or other aspects of management good or bad in this particular organization. Most often, consultants of many sorts apply this maturity measurement by conducting various expensive assessments, diagnostics or audits. It's funny that the least mature consultants are more likely to use maturity models, providing their unfortunate customers with recommendations like *"improve the maturity of all processes at least to the Level 3 of five"*. In contrast to this practice, some other experts believe that maturity models, on the whole, are of little use: at best, they answer the question "where are we now?" but never "where should we be?", and therefore do not provide valuable information for decision making.

Nevertheless, many people really want to understand: do we work well? Do we work better than others? What would the gurus say? Are we lagging behind or overtaking others? Fortunately, no generally accepted maturity model for DevOps have emerged yet. So, to satisfy this demand, we developed the following nearly meaningless test. It is intended to show how close your IT organization is to the ideal DevOps state.

Answer all questions honestly by choosing one of the options and then sum up your points.

1. We regularly measure the Lead Time, Process Time and the Percentage of work done without errors (% C/A):
   a. for all changes — 5 points
   b. from time to time — 3 points
   c. this is not measured, but we measure a lot of other things — 1 point
   d. all measurements are evil and provocation — 0 points

2. Our Lead time on average is:
   a. several hours — 5 points
   b. several days — 3 points
   c. several weeks — 1 point
   d. several months — 0 points

3. The frequency of releases to the production environment is:
    a. several times a day — 5 points
    b. several times a week — 3 points
    c. several times a month — 1 point
    d. we schedule releases on quarterly (or longer) basis — 0 points

4. We release:
    a. we do not release, our business does — 5 points
    b. as often as the business requires — 3 points
    c. usually rarely, but urgent releases are possible — 1 point
    d. in accordance with the release policy, when changes accumulate — 0 points

5. When we introduce changes to the production environment, the downtime is:
    a. there is no downtime — 5 points
    b. several minutes — 3 points
    c. several hours — 1 point
    d. we have a time agreed with the business to shut down the systems for change implementation — 0 points

6. We bring destruction to the production environment:
    a. we don't; it is done constantly by specially designed scripts and systems — 5 points
    b. when testing and deploying — 3 points
    c. almost every day, when we do the usual work — 1 point
    d. no destruction is possible, everything is stable — 0 points

7. We allocate time for improvements and innovations:
    a. up to 20% of working time — 5 points
    b. not regularly, but we are trying — 3 points
    c. we are getting better while doing the usual work — 1 point
    d. we are being improved by special people — 0 points

8. Our business experiments on living breathing users:
    a. every day — 5 points
    b. from time to time — 3 points
    c. when the IT department allows — 1 point
    d. we do not need to experiment, because our analysts know everything about the users perfectly well anyway — 0 points

9. Our deployment pipeline:
    a. works completely automatically — 5 points
    b. has several manual steps — 3 points

c. we do not have a pipeline — 1 point
   d. it is impossible to have a pipeline in our conditions — 0 points

10. We prioritize tasks in the value stream:
    a. based on the cost of delay — 5 points
    b. quickly calculating the benefits, resources and urgency — 3 points
    c. we play poker — 1 point
    d. we do not prioritize, this is done for us — 0 points

11. We deliver a minimum viable product (MVP) in order to:
    a. obtain the most complete information for decision making using minimum resources — 5 points
    b. understand whether it is worth moving on — 3 points
    c. show our beta version to the parties concerned — 1 point
    d. we do not deliver MVP — 0 points

12. We present system uptime information:
    a. on dedicated freely available web pages — 5 points
    b. in reports to individual customers — 3 points
    c. in the monitoring system — 1 point
    d. we do not present it — 0 points

13. We fix incidents in the production environment:
    a. by quickly re-creating part of the infrastructure — 5 points
    b. by rolling back unsuccessful changes — 3 points
    c. through the incident management process — 1 point
    d. by rebooting — 0 points

14. Our value stream:
    a. is visualized in a state of 'as is' and designed to 'to be' — 5 points
    b. is in our memory — 3 points
    c. is drawn on the wall in the manager's office — 1 point
    d. we (the IT department) are the value — 0 points

15. We update our IT infrastructure:
    a. only by means of the scripts stored in the version control system — 5 points
    b. by means of the scripts developed by the administrators for themselves — 3 points
    c. manually by the administrators — 1 point
    d. manually by the DevOps engineers — 0 points

There are 15 questions in the test; therefore, the maximum possible score is 75. We will assume that:
- if you scored up to 44 points: you have excellent prospects, eventually developing into new opportunities for integration with the labour market;
- if you scored from 45 to 74 points: you are on the right track, DevOps is close!
- if you scored 75 points: contact the author of the book immediately, he has some questions for you.

Appendix 2 Recommended reading

It turns out that there is nothing special to read among the hundreds of books already published by 2018 on DevOps. Many publications contain a very superficial view on the subject. Others focus on individual aspects of the phenomenon, not covering the entire width and not creating a coherent picture. A large number of very interesting books contains information on related issues, affecting DevOps only indirectly. Moreover, unfortunately, many books are notable for a rather modest ratio of the amount of useful information per number of pages.

Nevertheless, to have a deeper knowledge of DevOps, in addition to the publications referred before, I would like to point out the following:
1. Jez Humble, David Farley, *Continuous Delivery: Reliable Software Releases through Build, Test and Deployment Automation*, 2011, ISBN 978-0321601919
2. Gene Kim, Jez Humble, Patrick Debois, John Willis, *The Devops Handbook: How to Create Worldclass Agility Reliability and Security in Technology Organizations*, 2016, ISBN 978-1942788003
3. Paul Swartout, *Continuous Delivery and DevOps — A Quickstart Guide*, First published: November 2012, second edition: December 2014, ISBN 978-1784399313
4. Jennifer Davis, Katherine Daniels, *Effective DevOps - Building a Culture of Collaboration, Affinity, and Tooling at Scale*, 2016, O'Reilly Media, ISBN 978-1491926420

About the author

Oleg Skrynnik is a managing partner at Cleverics.

Oleg has been working in IT for more than twenty years, and more than fifteen on management positions. He is experienced in establishing and transforming IT departments of several large companies: financial institutions; manufacturing enterprises; service providers. He applies this professional experience in consulting projects and shares the lessons learned with attendees of his training, master-classes and business simulations.

Co-founder of itSMF Russia, Oleg is a recognized author and speaker. Apart from other publications, he has a blog on the popular RealITSM.ru portal.

Oleg's articles were awarded a First prize at the *ITSM in Russia* award in 2014 and 2017.

His professional competence is formally confirmed by a number of certificates:
- EXIN DevOps Master
- ITIL® Expert
- IT Service Manager
- Microsoft® Certified Systems Engineer
- Accredited GamingWorks™ Trainer

Index

-
20% tax   72
%C/A   38

A
A/B testing   51
Agile   33
agile approach   6
Agile coach   26
Agile Manifesto   5
Andon (Lean)   33
antifragile systems   19
anti-fragility   69
automation   25

B
Backlog   23
Beck, Kent   4
Blue-Green Deployments   51

C
Cagan, Marty   76
Canary Releases   51
Cattle versus Pets   53
CD3, Cost of Delay Divided by Duration   77
Chaos Monkey   20
cloud computing technology   8
CMDB, Configuration Management Database   95
containerization   10
Cost of Delay   77
COTS, Commercial Off-the-Shelf   87
Cunningham, Ward   17

D
Dark Launches   44
Debois, Patrick   19

deployment pipeline   40
DevOps engineer   26

E
Enterprise lean management   75
extreme programming (XP)   4

F
Farley, David   43
flow   40, 59
Fowler, Martin   17
fragile   18

G
Goldratt, Eliyahu   40

H
hackathon   73
HiPPO   63
Humble, Jez   19, 43
hypothesis evaluation   15

I
IDE, Integrated Development Environment   88
incident   52
intangibility   33
IT infrastructure as code   7

J
just-in-time (JIT)   33

K
Kaizen Blitz   72
Kanban   23, 60
Kim, Gene   19
Kurzweil, Ray   14

L

Law of Accelerating Returns 14
Lead Time 38
Lean 29
LTS, Long Term Support 83

M

microservice architecture 91
Muri, Mura and Muda 29
MVP, Minimum Viable Product 75

N

NFR, non-functional requirements 68

O

Ohno, Taiichi 29
OR, operational requirements 68

P

pipeline 42
Planning Poker 76
Poppendieck, Mary and Tom 29
Process Time 38
product owner 68
program increment 72
pull system 61, 64

R

refactoring 18
Reinertsen, Don 77
release 49, 50
Ries, Eric 76

S

SAFe (Scaled Agile Framework) 23
Schwaber, Ken 4
Scrum 34, 68

Scrum Master 26
Shadow Release 44
Shift left testing 70
Simian Army 20
Single-piece Flow 66
SLA, Service Level Agreement 94
SOA, Service-Oriented Architecture 90

T

Taleb, Nassim 19
Technology Radar 71
Test Impact Analysis 42
Theory of constraints 40
time to market 13
Toyota 29

V

value stream 37
value stream mapping 38
version control systems 44
virtualization 7
Virtual Private Network (VPN) 8

W

waste 29
waterfall model 3
Water-scrum-fall 76
Wegermann, Marcel 21
Willis, John 19
WIP Limit 64

Y

You built it, you run it 96

Z

Zero-Downtime Releases 51